CONTENTS

Helion & Company Limited
Unit 8 Amherst Business Centre
Budbrooke Road
Warwick
CV34 5WE
England
Tel. 01926 499 619
Email: info@helion.co.uk
Website: www.helion.co.uk
Twitter: @helionbooks
Visit our blog https://helionbooks.wordpress.com/

Typeset by Mach 3 Solutions (www.mach3solutions.co.uk)
Cover design by Paul Hewitt, Battlefield Design (www.battlefield-design.co.uk)

ISBN 978-1-804519-11-0

British Library Cataloguing-in-Publication Data
A catalogue record for this book is available from the British Library

We always welcome receiving book proposals from prospective authors.

To Suzanne and Arno

Note: In order to simplify the use of this book, all names, locations and geographic designations are as provided in *The Times World Atlas*, or other traditionally accepted major sources of reference, as of the time of described events.

ABBREVIATIONS AND ACRONYMS

AAM	air-to-air missile
AFZ	Air Force of Zimbabwe
BAF	Bangladesh Air Force (*Bangladesh Biman Bahini*)
CATIC	China National Aero-Technology Import and Export Corporation
CKD	component knock-down (kits)
DoD	Department of Defense (US)
DPRK	Democratic People's Republic of Korea (North Korea)
FASh	Albanian Air Force (*Forcat Ushtarake Ajrore Shqipetare*)
HUD	Head-up Display
IRIAF	Islamic Republic of Iran Air Force (*Niruye Havayi Jomhuriye Islamiye Iran*)
JWTZ	Tanzanian Air Force Command
KPAAF	Korean People's Army Air Force
LTTE	Liberation Tigers of Tamil Eelam
MANPADS	Man-Portable Air Defence System
NAF	Nigerian Air Force
OCU	Operation Conversion Unit
PAC	Pakistan Aeronautical Complex
PAF	Pakistan Air Force (Pakistan *Fiza'ya*)
RWR	radar warning receiver
SLAF	Sri Lanka Air Force
TFB	tactical fighter base
USA	United States of America
USSR	Union of Soviet Socialist Republics
USAF	United States Air Force

ACKNOWLEDGEMENTS

The author's special thanks go to Guido E. Bühlmann for his unique photographic material and Stefan Büttner and Alexander Golz for their magnificent photos, as well as for their many years of travelling with me. The author would like to express his sincere thanks to Andy Miles at Helion, whose patience and understanding ultimately made a lengthy and challenging project a success.

Furthermore, the author would like to thank all those who have contributed in any way to the creation of this book – be it through contributions, pictures, texts, books or by opening doors:

Wing Commander Asad, Air Marshal Muhammad Enamul Bari, Winston Brent, Victor Bertschi, dlsunshy, Dr Jakub Fojtik, Siegmar Frenzel, Marcus Fülber, Major Hadushi, Air Vice Marshal M. Naim Hassan, Group Captain M.D. Shaharul Huda, Wing Commander Mahmud Mehedi Hussain, Group Captain M. Saeedul Hassan Khan, First Lieutenant Shkelzen Krypi, Lieutenant Colonel Kuleci, Awais Lali, Lieutenant Colonel (GS) Holger Leukert, Colonel Lleshaj, Lieutenant Colonel Lleshi, Chris Lofting, Ian Malcom, Group Captain Abidemi Timothy Marquis, Matthias Muth, Air Commodore M. Mafidur Rahman, Air Commodore Mohammad Obaidur Rahman, Mohammad Razzazan, Andreas Rupprecht, Air Commodore Sarfraz Ahmed Khan, Ulrich Schneider, Lieutenant Colonel (GS) Carlo G. Schnell, Erik Sleutelberg, Kai Spörhase, Lukáš Syrovy, Babak Taghvaee, Dr István Toperczer, Jiří Vaněk, Alan Warnes, Marc van Zon.

INTRODUCTION

The first volume of this publication described the development history of the Chinese MiG-21, from the licensed production of the Soviet original to further development with Western assistance and finally to independent Chinese concepts. The second volume focuses on the use of the export versions of the J-7 on four continents, two of which – Europe and North America – play only an exotic outsider role. In Europe, Albania, which was almost politically isolated, received just 12 J-7s (or MiG-21F-13s assembled in China). In North America, a similarly modest number of F-7s served as realistic enemy simulators for the US Air Force. The clear focus of the F-7/FT-7's deployment is on Asia and Africa, where 13 user countries are located. South America could have been added to the list of continents if the two interested parties there – Argentina and Brazil – had not decided against Chinese aircraft.

The first volume already illustrated that the requirements of the purchasing countries have had a decisive influence on the development of the aircraft family. Pakistan in particular, which relies almost entirely on Chinese weapons, has had a significant influence on the evolution of the F-7/FT-7 family, not only with its demanding specifications, but also with technology transfer and active participation in testing. The role of the user countries in the development process will not be discussed again in the second volume. The description is limited to which versions were delivered in what quantities and at what time. For technical details, please refer to the first volume.

Looking at the user countries, similarities and differences become apparent. Some – Egypt, Bangladesh, Iraq, the Democratic People's Republic of Korea (DPRK, North Korea), Nigeria, Tanzania and the USA – had previously operated Soviet-made MiG-21s. Egypt, Iraq, the DPRK and the USA operated or operate both models in parallel. For others, such as Iran or Zimbabwe, the procurement of the F-7 represents their first ever contact with Soviet-Chinese technology. And while Sri Lanka made a successful re-entry into jet aviation with the F-7, it is Namibia's first ever jet fighter aircraft.

As in the first volume, the author has attempted to rely on first-hand material. In Pakistan and Bangladesh, he had the opportunity to visit air bases and gain an impression of their daily operations. In Albania, unfortunately, the visit took place at a time when the J-7s were no longer flying. In Iran, Nigeria and Sri Lanka, public events provided some insight, and in Egypt, a secret peek over the fence was possible. For all other countries, it was necessary to rely on third-party material and

The author on an FT-5 during a visit to PAF Air Base Mianwali in 2004. (Stefan Büttner)

publicly available sources. It is noteworthy that for only one of the countries in question – Pakistan – a fairly detailed account of its air force history is available, but even there, the F/FT-7 is only covered sparsely. In all other cases, an attempt was made to create roughly equally structured descriptions from the available information, consisting of a brief history, the process and scope of procurement, operational history, a list of losses and an outlook.

Although the F-7 versions based on the J-7G, the associated FT-7 two-seaters and, above all, the FTC-2000 are relatively new aircraft, the fleets have already shrunk significantly in recent years. On the one hand, Pakistan, as the largest operator, has replaced most of the F-7s in its operational squadrons with JF-17s and relegated the remaining aircraft to training roles. On the other hand, the fleets of some user countries, such as Nigeria, Myanmar and Sudan, have suffered significant losses due to both combat operations and accidents. Nevertheless, there is a good chance that at least some F/FT-7s will still be flying in the next decade.

Just like the first volume, the second is not meant to be the final word on the topic, but rather a starting point for discussion to get more insights. The author welcomes feedback from readers – comments, additions, and questions. You can reach the author at holger.mueller@mig-21.de.

The author in conversation with the then Chief of Air Staff of the Bangladesh Air Force, Air Marshal Muhammad Enamul Bari. (Stefan Büttner)

1

ALBANIA

Founded on 24 April 1951 at Tirana Air Base, the *Forcat Ushtarake Ajrore Shqipetare* (FASh – Albanian Air Force) had to be created de facto from scratch, as there had previously been no Albanian military aviation. Initially, its development was supported by the USSR.

After the Soviet-Chinese rift in 1961, Albania broke off relations with the Soviet Union, making China the sole supplier of armaments. As a result, China stepped up its support for Albania, which had been ongoing since the early 1950s, including free military aid.

Component knock-down kits (CKD) of 12 J-7s built or assembled in Shenyang arrived at Durrës port in November 1970. As already noted in the first volume of this publication, it could not yet be conclusively clarified whether the aircraft were actually the exact copy of the MiG-21F-13 designated as J-7 or whether they were CKD of this type delivered from the Soviet Union and assembled in China. While the personnel called the aircraft 'MiG-21', technical documents referred to them as 'Type 7'. The latter was the reason for the subsequent use of the designation J-7.

Chinese technicians assembled the aircraft. In December 1970, the first aircraft was test-flown by a Chinese pilot. One month later, an Albanian pilot flew the J-7 for the first time. It is remarkable that China was giving up around a third of the available fleet of its most modern fighter aircraft at this time. Possible explanations are that no other type in the Chinese inventory could have met Albanian demand (neighbouring countries Yugoslavia, Greece and Italy already had Mach 2 types) and that China considered the mini-fleet to be of little value.

Originally serving with the Tirana-Rinas-based *7594 Regjiment*, from 1974 the J-7s serialled 0201 to 0207, 0209, 0210 and 0304 (the serials of the two aircraft that later crashed are not known) formed the first squadron of the *5646 Regjiment*, which also had two squadrons of F-6s (MiG-19s). The main task of this unit was defence against the arch-enemy, Yugoslavia. Gjadër Air Base, around 70km north of Tirana, was built from 1969 onwards for this regiment. On 10 July 1973, a J-7 landed on the runway there for the first time. After previously delivered Soviet MiG-19PMs were exchanged for Chinese aircraft, the J-7s armed with PL-2s were the only missile-carrying aircraft in the Albanian fleet.

The political reforms in China after the death of Mao prompted the Albanian dictator Enver Hoxha to break off relations with the People's Republic in 1978 and thus with his only remaining ally. After the Albanian-Sino split, the FASh did not procure any new systems at all. Since the People's Republic of China was also the most important supplier of spare parts, it was only possible to ensure the operational readiness of the fleet thanks to extensive self-sufficiency. As early as the 1970s, the repair facility in Kuçovë became capable of carrying out complete major overhauls of the most important types and took over the engine overhauls that had previously been carried out in China. Through covert purchases of technology on the world market (among others from Sweden), capacities for the manufacture of spare parts and engine components were built up for most aircraft types, but not for the J-7. As a result, the J-7s flew much less frequently than the rest of the fleet. By the time they were retired, individual aircraft had only spent between 300 and 600 hours in the air.

Before the break with Beijing, the Albanian J-7 pilots received their training in China. Between 1978 and 1990, training took place

Operations from the flightline at an unidentified airfield. If the picture was taken in Gjadër, the control tower in the background fell victim to the riots of 1997. It is noteworthy that the pilot of the J-7 is wearing leather headgear and not the usual Chinese helmet. (FASh, Repro Stefan Büttner)

Pilots prepare for training flights in Gjadër. The rock in the background is part of the mountain massif into which a tunnel was bored to accommodate the aircraft. Pilots and aircraft stand in front of one of the two tunnel entrances. (FASh, Repro Stefan Büttner)

Only a few colour photographs exist of J-7s with the old national emblem bearing a red star in the centre. This had been replaced by two concentric red circles separated by a black one. The picture is also rare because it shows an aircraft outside the Gjadër tunnel. (Open source)

The Albanian J-7s spent most of their lives underground, leaving the tunnel in Gjadër only for their rare flights. Within 30 years, the aircraft had completed just 300 to 600 flight hours, although it cannot be ruled out that they had already flown a few hours when they were delivered from China. (Stefan Büttner)

With the decision to decommission them, all work on the J-7s was stopped and the aircraft remained in their then condition, such as the 0304 with its tail removed. (Holger Müller)

In the 1990s, the Federal Republic of Germany provided Albania with F, F2S and F2SK versions of the R11 engine from the stocks of the dissolved East German Air Force. Only this made it possible to continue flight operations until the early 2000s. (Holger Müller)

with the regiment in Gjadër. Two of the aircraft were lost in service. One crashed on 12 June 1974 – before the transfer to Gjadër – due to a technical fault, while a second aircraft fell victim to a bird strike during take-off on 28 March 1982. The remaining 10 aircraft survived both the end of communism in Albania and the civil war-like revolts of the following years.

The political transition that began in Albania with the death of dictator Hoxha in 1985 opened up new markets for the procurement of defence equipment, but the country lacked the funds to purchase just the most basic components. Even maintaining the status quo was only possible with some compromises. As early as 1990, the training of new pilots on the J-7 was discontinued, as the available resources were barely sufficient to keep the already qualified pilots proficient. Flight operations could only be maintained thanks to the delivery of numerous MiG-21 engines by the Federal Republic of Germany in the early 1990s. The engines from former German Democratic Republic stocks replaced the unreliable Chinese ones.

As a result of the unrest in 1997, the FASh's aircraft fleet suffered massive losses from which it would never recover. Numerous airfields, including Gjadër, were stormed by mobs and the facilities and aircraft found there were destroyed.

Only by mobilising all remaining resources were the FASh's J-7 able to carry out a number of flights in 1998 as a deterrent against airspace violations by Yugoslav aircraft and to take part in the air parade to mark the 90th anniversary of the Albanian army in 2002. As part of the reorganisation of the Albanian air force, which began in 2002, all operational Albanian aircraft, including the J-7, were concentrated at the Rinas base near Tirana. On 2 December of the same year, a J-7 took-off from there for the last time for a short flight.

A modernisation of the J-7 allegedly negotiated with Romania was never actually planned. At the end of 2005, the Albanian government, realistically assessing its own capabilities, decided to decommission all fixed-wing aircraft, thereby dashing all hopes of pilots and technicians for a second life for the Mach 2 fighters. The Minister of Defence also refused to grant the personnel's wish to carry out a farewell flight on the occasion of Air Force Day on 24 April 2006. At this time, one pilot still held a valid type-licence. One of the two aircraft finally operational and parked in Rinas is now on display in the Army Museum in Tirana (0209), the other (0207) was scuttled as a diving object near Dhëmi. Of the eight other aircraft, one is on display in Kuçovë (0203), while seven may be still in Gjadër aircraft tunnel.

2

ARGENTINA AND BRAZIL

With the availability of the F-7M with Western avionics, China was hoping for export opportunities among users of Western technology looking for alternatives due to the lack of funds or existing sanctions. Two possible candidates had been identified in Brazil and Argentina.

In December 1986, a Brazilian delegation of two pilots and four technicians travelled to China to evaluate the F-7M. After several days of evaluation on the ground, a short flight test followed on the 22nd of the month. The Brazilians judged the F-7M to be comparable to the Mirage III and F-5E models currently in service with the *Força Aérea Brasileira*, although the Chinese model was said to have advantages in terms of avionics.

China submitted an offer for 30 aircraft, including training, spare parts and armament for US$160 million, whereby the Brazilian request for the installation of a Western ejection seat (Martin-Baker) was accepted. However, an offer made by the USA in 1988 to supply 22 used F-5Es and four F-5Fs for only US$113 million thwarted Chinese efforts to win the sale.

Shortly afterwards, in April 1987, an Argentinian delegation consisting of two technicians and five pilots travelled to China to also test the F-7M. After the losses in the Falklands War, the Argentinian air force was looking for a cheap replacement from new sources, as the previous suppliers were no longer available due to existing embargoes. During a 40-day stay, two of the Argentinian pilots tested both the F-7M and the JJ-7.

The subsequent assessment was worse than that of the Brazilians: according to the pilots, the F-7 did not represent any progress compared to the current Argentinian models (A-4 Skyhawk, Mirage III/IAI Dagger). The robustness and favourable price were rated positively, but this was relativised by the extensive changes required in operating procedures and maintenance. Finally, Argentina itself lacked the means to procure this favourable type, so that the purchase of the F-7 ultimately came to nothing.

Argentinian pilots in the cockpit of a JJ-7 during flight testing. The absence of paintwork and any markings on the aircraft is noteworthy. (Open source)

Group photo of the Argentine pilots with their Chinese instructors. The prototype of the F-7M with the Head-up-display in the cockpit represents the current state of development at that time. (Open source)

3

BANGLADESH

The birth of the Bangladeshi nation was closely linked to the MiG-21. During the war of liberation of the former East Pakistan against its motherland, MiG-21s spearheaded the Indian Air Force fighting against Pakistani armed forces. After a short but extremely bloody war, Bangladesh gained independence on 26 March 1971 with Indian support.

Under Prime Minister Mujibur Rahman, the country – allied with India – pursued a pro-Soviet course. As a result, the Bangladesh Air Force (BAF, *Bangladesh Biman Bahini*) received 20 MiG-21MFs and two MiG-21UMs from the USSR in 1973. The aircraft were deployed at Tezgaon base near Dhaka, which had been modernised with Soviet assistance. At the same time, the USSR sent military advisors to the country to support the development of the air force, while the future Bangladeshi pilots spent time in India for training.

According to Soviet plans, Bangladesh was to be expanded as an outpost against the growing Chinese influence in the region. These plans were thwarted by a coup d'état in which the founder of the state, Mujibur Rahman, was killed. Under army chief Ziaur Rahman, who prevailed in the subsequent power struggles, the country turned towards China.

As the readiness of the MiG-21 fleet continued to decline at the end of the 1980s – mainly due to climatic conditions, but also due to a shortage of spare parts – it was China that delivered replacements in October (according to other sources in December) 1989 with 16 F-7MBs and three FT-7BBs – the BAF's most modern aircraft at the time. The F-7MBs were given the serials 1413–1428, the FT-7BBs the numbers 2429–2431 and were equipped with PL-7 air-to-air missiles

F-7MB of No. 35 Squadron 'Thundercats' at Dhaka-Kurmitola base. At the time the photograph was taken, the aircraft was no longer in delivery condition but had already been fitted with a Martin-Baker ejection seat. (Holger Müller collection)

The first exported two-seaters, including the FT-7BB for Bangladesh, are largely identical to the JJ-7s used by the PLAAF. Modifications to the airframe and equipment were only integrated later at customer's request. (Holger Müller collection)

(AAMs) and 57-2 and 90-1 unguided rockets. Unlike most F-7M variants, the F-7MB could carry a reconnaissance pod, although this was rarely used. Further two-seaters followed in 1991 (one, serial 2432), 1999 (three, 2433–2435) and 2002 (one, 2436). In 2007, a second-hand JJ-7A (2437) was delivered, which differed from the other aircraft in terms of its equipment. It is possible that the aircraft delivered between 1999 and 2002 were JJ-7As too, as stretched two-seaters were usually exported at this time. Upon delivery, the F-7MB and at least the first few FT-7BBs had the HTY-2 ejection seat, while the JJ-7A was equipped with Chinese HTY-6E seats.

With the aircraft delivered in 1989, No. 35 Squadron 'Thundercats' was set up on 28 March 1990 at the Kurmitola base. The unit is still stationed there today on the military side of Dhaka-Zia International Airport (now Hazrat Shahjalal). The base itself had since been renamed Bangabandhu and is also home to No. 5 Squadron 'Supersonics', with which the Thundercats shared the aircraft for a long time.

In the background of this photo from the early days of the F-7MB's service, the aircraft's original configuration with the HTY-2 ejection seat can be seen. (BAF, Repro Holger Müller)

An F-7MB with maximum payload, consisting of a 720-litre drop-tank on the fuselage pylon, two 490-litre drop-tanks on the outer wing pylons and two HF-5A rocket pods on the inner wing pylons, taxis the runway for take-off. (Alexander Golz)

Take-off of two F-7MBs from Dhaka-Bangabandhu. Both aircraft are equipped with three 490-litre drop-tanks and HF-5A rocket pods. (Alexander Golz)

At around the same time as the new F-7 generation was delivered, the F-7MBs were at least partially upgraded to match them in terms of equipment – recognisable by new antennas under the cockpit and on the vertical stabiliser. (Alexander Golz)

Both the FT-7BB in front and the F-7MB behind feature the extended antenna equipment of the modernised aircraft. While the two-seater carries the communications-antenna on the back of the fuselage, the single-seater has it under the cockpit. (Alexander Golz)

Although eight MiG-29s were procured in the meantime, Bangladesh ordered 12 F-7BGs and four FT-7BGs on 25 June 2005. In February 2006, the Bangladeshi Defence Minister informed the parliament about this purchase. Prior to this, the BAF had sent pilots to Chengdu Aircraft Corporation to test the type. After their transfer by Bangladeshi pilots from Kunming (China) via Mandalay (Myanmar) to Kurmitola, the F-7BGs (F932–F943) and FT-7BGs (F944–F947) were commissioned with No. 5 Squadron on 4 April 2006. This was preceded by the signing of a contract for the procurement of spare parts and component overhaul between the BAF and Pakistan Aeronautical Complex (PAC) Kamra on 19 March 2006. The F-7BG is primarily used for air defence. Its secondary tasks are air-to-ground operations and reconnaissance. However, it does not have a special reconnaissance pod for the latter.

Finally, in 2011 Bangladesh ordered 12 and four aircraft of the ultimate versions F-7BG-I and FT-7BG-I, respectively. The aircraft, which were given the serials 2711–2722 and 2701–2704 respectively, were delivered between 2012 and 2013 and equip No. 35 Squadron.

After the arrival of the F-7BG-I and FT-7BG-I, the F-7MB and FT-7BB were handed over to No. 25 Squadron 'Trendsetters' in Zahurul Hague, on the southern outskirts of Chittagong. There they are used for advanced training (operational conversion units, OCUs) as well as in the secondary role for air defence.

Photo taken upon the arrival of the F-7BG and FT-7BG in Bangladesh. The aircraft were flown by BAF pilots from Kunming in China via Mandalay in Myanmar to Kurmitola. (BAF, Repro Holger Müller)

F-7BG landing in Dhaka-Bangabandhu. Two 490-litre drop-tanks under the wings are standard equipment for Bangladeshi aircraft in daily flight operations. The transfer range in this configuration is a good 1,700 kilometres, with a possible flight time of just under two hours. Nevertheless, the aircraft usually remain in the air for only one hour. (Holger Müller)

An FT-7BG rolls to take-off along the roofed flightline at Dhaka-Bangabandhu, which provides protection from the tropical sun. The aircraft belongs to No. 5 Squadron, whose name was originally 'Supersonics' but has since been changed to 'Defenders'. (Holger Müller)

In the background behind the FT-7BG rolling off the runway, the terminal of Hazrat Shahjalal International Airport can be seen, with which the two F-7 squadrons No. 5 and No. 35 as well as the MiG-29 squadron No. 8 share the infrastructure. (Holger Müller)

FT-7BG on take-off. The slotted flaps, extended to 25 degrees, are clearly visible. (Holger Müller)

As part of the recent overhauls, the paintwork of the F-7BG has adapted to match that of the F-7BG-I. Apart from the serials, the versions can be distinguished by different antenna equipment and the left cannon of the BG, which is missing on the BG-I. (Alexander Golz)

The armament of the F-7BG/BG-I consists of PL-5EII and PL-9C missiles, satellite-guided bombs with LS-6 guidance kit (BG-I only), 250-kilogram and 500-kilogram bombs, anti-runway Durandal penetration bombs, BL755 cluster bombs and 90mm calibre unguided rockets. Both the F-7MB and the F-7BG were retrofitted for target towing.

The eight or so F-7MBs still in service were fitted with Global Positioning System receivers. The FT-7BBs received new equipment, including modern head-up displays (HUDs). Externally, the modernised aircraft can be recognised by their additional antennas. In addition, the original HTY-2 ejection seat of the F-7MB and FT-7BB has been replaced by the Martin-Baker Mk.10L. In 2019, a corresponding contract was signed between the BAF and the British manufacturer, which also included the establishment of a local maintenance centre. Apparently, Martin-Baker seats had also been installed in Bangladeshi F/FT-7s before.

There are confirmed loss reports for six F-7MBs: 1428 crashed on 23 September 2010 and 1416 on 29 June 2015. The fate of four other aircraft (1415, 1420, 1423, and 1425) is unknown, meaning that these aircraft could probably be assigned to the losses reported for 4 September 1994, 26 October 1998, 7 June 2005 and 8 April 2008. Of the FT-7Bs, two aircraft – 2433 on 7 January 2001 and 2430 on 25 February 2003 – were decommissioned due to accidents. The wreckage of the latter aircraft is stored at Dhaka-Bashar base.

According to Turkish sources, Bangladesh had signed a contract for the delivery of TEBER control kits from the manufacturer Roketsan in 2021. The kits are used to convert Mk.81 and Mk.82 free-fall bombs into guided bombs. They are intended to equip the F-7BGs, which, unlike the F-7BG-I, do not have a precision bombing capability ex works. Corresponding integration tests have been underway since 2019.

The F/FT-7BGs have since been overhauled and the original blue livery replaced by a grey one similar to that of the F-7BG-I. The F-7BG F932 crashed at the Rasulpur Firing Range on 23 November 2018, killing the pilot. When the FT-7BG-I 2701 crashed into a school in Dhaka on 21 July 2025, the pilot and more than 30 people on the ground were killed and more than 100 were injured. Despite these losses, both the F/FT-7BG and F/FT-7BG-I are expected to remain in service for some time to come.

Like the F/FT-7BG before them, the F/FT-7BG-I were transferred by Bangladeshi pilots. The flights took place over several months from late 2012 to mid-2013. (BAF, Repro Holger Müller)

An F-7BG-I over the typical vast swamps of Bangladesh. Thanks to the comparatively small size of the country, of 500km each in north-south and east-west direction, the F-7s based centrally in Dhaka can cover the entire airspace. (BAF)

The wing tip visible in the image indicates that the photo was taken from a two-seater aircraft with a classic delta wing. The F-7BG-I in the foreground is carrying PL-5 training missiles. (BAF)

From this perspective, the difference between the original delta shaped wing of the FT-7BG-I in front and the double-delta wing of the two F-7BG-I behind it is clearly visible. (BAF)

An F-7BG-I lands at Dhaka-Bangabandhu with a brake chute. Unlike the MiG-21, the J/F-7 uses only brake chutes with round canopies. (Holger Müller)

Flight preparation of an F-7BG-I. The engine is started using a battery cart. (Holger Müller)

Upon signal from ground crew, an FT-7BG-I drops its brake chute. It is then recovered, repacked and reused. In principle, taxiing is also possible with the brake chute, but this causes increased wear on the chute canopy and ropes. (Holger Müller)

The take-off performance of the BG-I two-seaters is comparable to that of the single-seaters. However, in terms of landing speed and low-speed characteristics, the single-seaters have clear advantages thanks to their double-delta wings. (Holger Müller)

F-7BG-I takes off from Dhaka-Bangabandhu. Thanks to the relatively low weight, combined with the powerful WP-13FI engine, the climb performance is impressive, even in the tropical climate of Bangladesh. (Holger Müller)

An F-7BG-I taxis back to the flightline after landing. The upwardly opened door of the brake chute container indicates that the brake chute was used and then released. (Holger Müller)

4

EGYPT

After General Nasser came to power in 1952 and Egypt gained independence from Great Britain, the country pursued a course of rapprochement with the USSR and its allies, which not only influenced the country's foreign policy until the early 1970s, but also resulted in massive deliveries of technology from socialist states. From the early 1960s, this also included Soviet-built MiG-21s.

Several hundred of them were deployed by the *Al Quwwat al Jawwiya al Gomhouriya al Arabiye* (the Air Force of the United Arab Republic, as the state was known between 1958 and 1972) and *Al Quwwat al Jawwiya il-Misriya* (Egypt Air Force, EAF) during the Six-Day War in 1967, the inter-war period and the Yom Kippur War of 1973.

The expulsion of Soviet advisors ordered by then Egyptian President Sadat in July 1972 halted the further influx of Soviet technology. When, after initial successes on the Arab side, Israel regained the upper hand in the Yom Kippur War and the losses, especially for the Egyptians, increased, the USSR resumed its arms deliveries. These continued until the summer of 1974 and included further MiG-21s. The final disagreement ended MiG-21 deliveries permanently.

In order to keep its MiG-21 fleet operational and compensate for the losses, the Egyptian government asked China in January 1979 for help with the procurement of aircraft, engines and spare parts. After lengthy negotiations, Egypt and the China National Aero-Technology Import and Export Corporation (CATIC) signed a contract on 5 April 1980 for the export of 60 F-7s as well as engines, spare parts and test equipment with a total value of over US$200 million. In return, Egypt supplied MiG-21MF and MiG-21US pattern aircraft for the development of the J-7III and JJ-7.

The first 20 F-7As arrived in Egypt in late 1981, early 1982 and were assigned serials 4501–4520. The second batch of 40 (modified) F-7As – externally similar to the F-7B – was delivered by the end of 1982 and received serials 4521–4560. In 1977, Egypt ordered 180 R.550 Magic AAMs from France, which were delivered between 1980 and 1983. A further 120 of an order placed in 1983 followed in 1986–87. The wiring of the second batch F-7As was modified for the use of these missiles, which meant a considerable increase in combat effectiveness.

According to various sources, part of the Egyptian F-7 fleet was passed on to Iraq. This is said to have been part of a 1981 contract for arms deliveries worth US$800 million.

Between 1981 and 1997, F-7s equipped the 25 and 26 Tactical Fighter Squadrons of the 102 Tactical Fighter Wing in Fayid, east

With no Chinese two-seaters available when the Egyptian F-7s were delivered, Soviet two-seaters such as this MiG-21UM were used in the operational units. (Holger Müller)

of Cairo and close to the Suez Canal. Their main task was advanced training. Later, all remaining aircraft were pooled in the 26 Tactical Fighter Squadron at Hurghada Air Base by the Red Sea, where they remained in the training role until 2015 and then were transferred to the reserve.

In the early 1980s, the Egyptian MiG-21s were subject of various modernisation programmes carried out with Western assistance. This included the fitting of HUDs, new radar warning receivers (RWRs) as well as Magic and Sidewinder missiles, chaff and flare dispensers, identification friend-or-foe (IFF) devices and jamming pods. It is not known to what extent the F-7s were also involved.

At least two F-7s are on display today as monuments in Cairo West and Marsa Matruh.

Although the specified service life of the first export version, the F-7A, is quite short, the aircraft flew in the training role with the Egypt Air Force until around 2015. (Holger Müller)

F-7B in formation flight. While images of the F-7A appeared repeatedly until the end of its service life, there are only a few images of the F-7B, which may be an indication of its alleged transfer to Iraq. (Open source)

An F-7A approaching Hurghada. The external appearance shows some signs of wear and tear, whereas there were no signs of upgrades such as additional antennas or other additions. (Jiří Vaněk)

Training operations in Hurghada regularly included low-level flights over the airfield in formations of two or even four aircraft. This picture clearly shows that the serials were applied in different sizes. (Jiří Vaněk)

Egyptian F-7A, photographed in Hurghada in 2008. At that time, the aircraft were only used for training purposes. The striking orange colour scheme is used on all Egypt Air Force aircraft types that are operated in neighbouring countries too. This is to prevent accidental shoot-downs. (Open source)

5

IRAQ

The overthrow of the Iraqi monarchy in July 1958 put an end to Anglo-American influence in the country and initiated its turn towards the USSR. However, a few more years and a number of coups d'état took place before the Ba'ath Party permanently took power under General al-Bakr in 1968. His successor as president was Saddam Hussein, who had held this office from 1979.

Immediately after the change of power, Soviet deliveries of armaments began, including MiG-21s. From 1962, No. 11 Squadron (the Iraqis had retained the British organisation of their flying units) of the *Al Quwwat al Jawwiya al Iraqiya* (Iraqi Air Force) was equipped with MiG-21F-13s. Numerous other units and almost all export versions of the MiG-21 followed. Their total number was likely to have reached several hundred. Iraqi MiG-21s fought in the wars with Israel in 1967 and 1973 and were also at the forefront of the war against Iran, which began in 1980.

During the war with Iran, the Iraqi air force suffered considerable losses of pilots and aircraft, which made replacement purchases of technology and the training of new personnel urgent. In view of the enormous costs of the war, Iraq was looking for low-cost options and found them in Chinese F-7s, although the information circulating about their procurement varies widely. According to Chinese sources, on 27 June 1981 the Kingdom of Jordan ordered 80 F-7s on behalf of Iraq at a price of more than US$200 million, delivered in two batches. The first 20 aircraft of the F-7B version were delivered to Jordan by November 1982 and later transferred to Iraq. All 60 further aircraft belonged to the F-7M version. These reached Jordan between July 1984 and May 1985, from where they were transferred to Iraq. The deliveries were completed with eight FT-7BI two-seaters, which were delivered to Iraq via Jordan from 13 June 1988. The single-seaters were given serials in the 215xx and 216xx range, the twin-seaters in the 210xx range.

According to other sources, the Iraqis received their first F-7Bs via Egypt. Reportedly, they arrived either at Gianaclis Air Base or at the Arab Organisation for Industrialisation Aircraft Factory (AOI/ACF) in Helwan, where they were assembled and test-flown by Chinese technicians and pilots and finally flown over to Iraq via Saudi Arabia. There were also reports that deliveries were made directly to Iraq. Egyptian technicians are said to have assisted the Iraqis in the assembly of the aircraft, which were delivered disassembled aboard Iraqi An-12s. Sometimes it has been stated that the F-7s were financed by Saudi Arabia. The fact that these aircraft did not cause any additional costs for the Iraqi state budget, which was already burdened by the war, could have been the reason why Iraq acquired these aircraft, which were significantly inferior to the MiG-21bis already in service.

No photographs of Iraqi F-7s in active service could be found so far. All available images show damaged aircraft, here an F-7B, after the US-led coalition invaded the country in 2003. (US DoD)

Iraqi F-7s – both the F-7B and the F-7M – are said to have been modified for use of the French R.550 Magic AAM, which Iraq procured for its Mirage F-1. As the F-7M could fire the identical PL-7, it is conceivable that no modifications were necessary or that the alleged Magic was in fact the Chinese equivalent. PL-2s were also delivered from China together with the F-7s.

The F-7s did not see combat in the war against Iran but was used exclusively for training purposes.

After the end of the first Gulf War, there was little time to replenish the arsenal. The invasion of Kuwait on 2 August 1990 was followed by a worldwide arms embargo and an attack by a coalition led by the USA. At the start of hostilities, there were between 100 and 150 MiG-21/F-7s in Iraqi stocks (separate figures are not available). As the F-7s were heavily outmatched by the enemy, the Iraqis tried to hide the aircraft instead of sending them into a hopeless battle. Thanks to skilful camouflage, fewer than 20 MiG-21/F-7s were destroyed on the ground. Thus, even after the cessation of hostilities, Iraq was likely to have had operational F-7s at its disposal. Whether these were actually still flying is not known.

During the second invasion by the USA and its allies in spring 2003, Iraqi aircraft, including the F-7s still available at the time, were no longer used at all. Before the war, the number of F-7s was said to have been 35. It is not known how many of these were destroyed in the fighting or by the Iraqis themselves. A number of more-or-less intact F-7s and FT-7s fell into the hands of the allied forces under US command.

Almost all of the F/FT-7s photographed showed damage to the glazing, but otherwise hardly any traces of combat operations, which indicate that the aircraft were deliberately rendered unusable. The missing pitot tube tip of this F-7M also suggests that the aircraft was no longer serviceable even before the invasion. (US DoD)

This FT-7BI in the sand at the edge of an Iraqi base survived the fighting largely unscathed and only 'lost' its main landing gear tyres. The tail of a MiG-25 can be seen next to the aircraft. (US DoD)

6

IRAN

As the USA's most important ally in the Gulf region, Iran received extensive supplies of American military technology during the reign of Shah Mohammad Reza Pahlavi. The country's strategic military importance and its financial strength made it possible for the Iranian Air Force to become one of the largest operators of the F-4 Phantom II and the only one outside the USA to fly the F-14 Tomcat.

Military cooperation with the USA ended abruptly with the Islamic Revolution in 1979. Advisors were withdrawn, spare parts were not delivered and orders were cancelled. Despite this, Iran managed to keep large parts of its flying arsenal operational and successfully deploy them in the war against Iraq.

In the war, the Iranians experienced the MiG-21 as a dangerous air opponent that achieved a high number of air victories and was also effective in the air-to-ground role. This assessment, but also the comparatively low price and the easy-to-manage technology, were the reasons why Iran began to procure MiG-21s shortly after the war. However, these were not intended for the *Niruye Havayi Jomhuriye Islamiye Iran* (IRIAF, Islamic Republic of Iran Air Force), but for the *Sepāh-e Pāsdārān-e Enghelāb-e Eslāmi* (Army of the Guardians of the Islamic Revolution, or Revolutionary Guards or Pasdaran for short), which was endeavouring to establish its own flying component.

The first attempt failed due to German reunification. The delivery of 12 MiG-21PFs and four MiG-21U-600s was agreed with the German Democratic Republic (East Germany) in 1988. Iranian pilots were trained by the *Luftstreitkräfte/Luftverteidigung der Nationalen Volksarmee* (East German Air Force/Air Defence) and two two-seaters were delivered to Iran, assembled and test-flown in Isfahan by representatives of the Dresden aircraft factory, but never commissioned. The government of the Federal Republic of Germany prevented the entire deal from being finalised and all other aircraft were scrapped in Germany.

At the same time, Iran turned to China. After other weapons systems such as missiles had already been procured from there, Iran initially ordered 14 F-7 single-seaters and four twin-seaters during a trip to China by then President Ali Khamenei in May 1989. The order was later expanded to 30 F-7Ns and 20 FT-7Ns. A group of Iranian pilots travelled to China for retraining. There they initially flew JJ-6s and JJ-7s before switching to the single-seat J-7II.

The first two-seaters to be delivered were FT-7Bs, which served as an interim solution until the 20 FT-7Ns based on the FT-7P were available. The latter was still under development at the time of delivery in October 1990. Unlike the FT-7B, the stretched two-

Parade formation of F-7Ns at the 5th Tactical Air Base in Omidiyeh. The last two digits of the serials have been obscured. (Open source)

seaters have an on-board cannon, which was of decisive importance for their planned use as weapons trainers.

Six FT-7Bs, serials 3-7701–3-7706, were transported from Chengdu to Isfahan by an Iran Air Boeing 747, assembled there by Chinese technicians and then transferred by Iranian pilots to the 5th Tactical Air Base in Omidiyeh. The next deliveries of 15 F-7Ns each followed in May 1991 and February 1992. The single-seaters, with serials most likely in the range between 3-7501 and 3-7530, are basically the equivalent of the F-7P, with all the Western avionics components used there being replaced by Chinese ones. The aircraft are wired for the use of US air-to-ground weapons (bombs and unguided rockets) available in Iran. PL-7 AAMs were delivered together with the aircraft.

The first of the 20 FT-7Ns (serials 3-7701–3-7706 were reassigned, plus the numbers up to 3-7720) arrived in 1992, so that the six FT-7Bs could be returned to the manufacturer. A final order in 1994 included a further six FT-7Ns (3-7721–3-7726), which were delivered in 1996 and formed the basis for the formation of the newly established 84th Combat Command Training Squadron (CCTS) at 8th Tactical Fighter Base (TFB) in Isfahan. The last FT-7N delivered, serial 3-7726, differed from the other aircraft in that it was equipped with an LJ-2 RWR and a chaff and flare dispenser between the two fins under the rear fuselage. China's offer to equip all aircraft with such self-protection systems was not accepted.

As part of a reorganisation of IRIAF pilot training in 1996, the 53rd CCTS was relocated from Omidiyeh to Isfahan. At that time, the unit had six F-7Ns (3-7503, 3-7504, 3-7523, 3-7527, 3-7528 and 3-7529) and 13 FT-7Ns (3-7706, 3-7714, 3-7716–3-7726). Six F-7Ns flew with the 84th CCTS, another 21 together with 13 FT-7s in the two remaining squadrons of the 5th TFB. After the 52nd TFS was also converted into a training unit, F-7Ns were now only in service with the 51st TFS.

A reorganisation of the Iranian Air Force carried out in 2008 led, among other things, to the closure of two air bases – including Omidiyeh – and their handover to the Pasdaran. The 51st Tactical Fighter Squadron and 52nd Tactical Training Squadron based there were disbanded and their 21 F-7Ns and nine FT-7Ns were transferred to the 8th TFB. Sometime later, the Quick Reaction Alert (QRA) in Omidiyeh was resumed. Three F-7Ns (sometimes also two F-7Ns and one FT-7N, the latter for pilot training), equipped with two PL-7C AAMs and two 490-litre drop-tanks, were based there. There is conflicting information about further developments. One source states that in 2019 the QRA ended in Omidiyeh and the last three F-7Ns were transferred back to Isfahan, another claims that later three squadrons with F-7s operated from there again.

In Isfahan, an FT-7N of the 84th CCTS armed with PL-7Cs was on QRA duty together with the F-14s based there for drone defence, visual and weather reconnaissance tasks.

The UN embargo imposed on Iran in 2007 meant the end of Chinese support for maintenance of the F/FT-7, which until then had been carried out by Iranian personnel under Chinese supervision. In 2010, the IRIAF therefore set up a special maintenance unit for the F/FT-7 at the 8th TFB. The engines are overhauled by a maintenance centre specialised in the WP-7 at Doshan-Tappeh Air Base in Tehran.

From around 2009, several F-7s were decommissioned and cannibalised in order to obtain spare parts for the FT-7. The shrinking of the fleet was accompanied by a decline in flight activities. The number of annual flights of the 84th CCTS is said to be around 800, while the 5th TFB carried out more than 1,400 in its most active years. The unit's main task is pilot training. After basic training on the PC-7, future combat pilots make 60 flights on the FT-7N before transitioning to their operational type. During the annual large-scale live firing exercises the FT-7Ns were often seen firing missiles and dropping bombs. Sometimes they were involved in testing new weapons, such as the Yasin Y-ER-300 satellite-guided bomb guidance kit developed in Iran for Mk.82 bombs.

Before the Israeli air strikes between June 13 and 23, 2025, the IRIAF still had 23 single-seater F-7Ns and 20 two-seater FT-7Ns, including non-operational aircraft. Three F-7Ns were involved in accidents up to 1996 alone due to technical and pilot errors, two more on 25 May 1997 and 6 July 2008, and one FT-7N (3-7718) was lost on 27 April 2016 due to an engine and hydraulic failure as a result of maintenance deficiencies. The pilots survived. Another one crashed on 2 June 2018 (3-7723) for unknown reasons. Here, too, the crew managed to eject. The most recent crash was that of an FT-7N on 24 May 2022, in which both crew members were killed.

Formation of three FT-7Ns at the annual Army Day parade in April 2017. The aircraft bear their serials in European numerals on the nose and in Arabic numerals on the vertical stabiliser. According to the encircled number on the vertical stabiliser, the aircraft in the foreground belongs to the 8th TFB in Isfahan, while the other two belong to the 5th TFB in Omidiyeh. The aircraft from Isfahan has new paintwork and the symbol of the 84th CCTS on the fuselage and vertical stabiliser. (Alexander Golz)

F-7s were involved in testing the Yasin Y-ER-300 satellite-guided bomb guidance kit (centre, with wings) developed in Iran for Mk.82 bombs. It can be assumed that such weapon systems will sooner or later be integrated into the regular arsenal of the Iranian F/FT-7. (Holger Müller)

FT-7N on approach to Tehran-Mehrabad. The 3-7716 sports its original delivery livery and carries two 490-litre drop-tanks under the wings.

The red and white 3-7718, which carries here a 720-litre drop-tank under the fuselage, was lost in a crash on 27 April 2016. (Mohammad Razzazan)

Whether and how many aircraft were destroyed by the Israeli air force is not yet known. According to reports from spring 2022, four F-7Ns and 10 FT-7Ns were in service with the 84th CCTS of the 8th TFB, while nine other F-7Ns and FT-7Ns were at the base's maintenance centre. If these aircraft were still there at the time of the Israeli airstrikes, losses cannot be ruled out, as Isfahan airport and the airbase there were among the targets of the attacks. This could also affect inactive aircraft that have either been parked or cannibalised for spare parts. These aircraft were to be made airworthy again in a modernisation programme under the name 'Shahid Erfanian' (named after a pilot who had a fatal accident in an F-7N during a military parade in 1995). A FT-7N was serving as a pattern aircraft in this programme. The aim was to increase the manoeuvrability and fighting power of the FT-7N in order to keep the aircraft in service for another two decades. According to unconfirmed reports, the project, which had been ongoing since 2012, originally comprised an aerodynamic modernisation of the existing FT-7N based on the Chinese JL-9 (FTC-2000), whereby the aircraft were to receive outer wing sections with reduced sweep and additional manoeuvring flaps. In addition, a redesign of the nose section with a fixed nose and lateral air intakes was allegedly planned to enable the installation of an Iranian pulse-Doppler radar, a copy of the Chinese JL-10G/SY-80. As this concept probably exceeded Iran's capabilities, a modified programme was created that was limited to structural revisions and equipping the cockpit with new head-up displays and – in the case of the two-seaters – three Iranian-made multifunctional displays each for the student and instructor. The first components had already produced in 2019, but due to a lack of funds, the first flight of a modified FT-7N planned for late 2021 has never taken place.

In view of the latest developments, it seems unlikely that Iran will invest any additional resources in the F-7 fleet. If a sufficient number of aircraft have survived the hostilities and no further strikes follow, it can be assumed that the Iranian F/FT-7s will remain in service in unchanged form for some time to come.

Three FT-7Ns line up for take-off at Tehran-Mehrabad. Here too, the photo was probably taken on Army Day. (Mohammad Razzazan)

The encircled 8 on the vertical stabiliser of the FT-7N 3-7721, which was exhibited at the Iranian Armed Forces Aerial Achievements Exhibition in Tehran in February 2019, refers to its home base in Isfahan, and the dragon emblem to the operating unit 85. TFS. (Holger Müller)

7

DEMOCRATIC PEOPLE'S REPUBLIC OF KOREA

After liberation from Japanese occupation by US troops in 1945, Korea was divided into a Soviet and a US occupation zone, from which the Democratic People's Republic of Korea (DPRK, North Korea) and the Republic of Korea (RoK, South Korea) emerged shortly afterwards. The DPRK under its 'Great Leader' Kim Il Sung was massively supported with Soviet and Chinese weapons technology from the very beginning, but especially during the Korean War from 1950 to 1953.

After the North Koreans were supplied with large numbers of the then ultra-modern MiG-15 during the war, they later received MiG-17s, MiG-19s and MiG-21s. Of the latter, the F-13, PFM and MF versions as well as various two-seaters were delivered. After the collapse of the eastern superpower, the DPRK then procured second-hand MiG-21bis from Kazakhstan.

Thanks to its close ties with neighbouring China, North Korea was also one of the first recipients of the J-7: not a special export version, but the J-7I 'three modifications'. In 1982, 40 examples of this variant, originally intended for Chinese domestic use only, were delivered to the Korean People's Army Air Force (KPAAF). This is remarkable as only 188 aircraft of this version were produced and it was the most modern aircraft in the People's Liberation Army Air Force's inventory at the time. In addition, North Korea received these aircraft as military aid, i.e. free of charge. None of the aircraft has the brake chute container on vertical tail root – an indication that the first J-7Is were produced without this feature and that the retrofitting of this version in China only took place when North Korea had already received its aircraft.

MiG-21F-13 and J-7I side by side on a flightline in North Korea. The serials of the Soviet-built aircraft are in the 300 range, those of the Chinese examples in the 700 range. Clearly visible is the left cannon with reinforced fuselage panelling on the J-7I compared to the Aluminium surface of the MiG-21F-13 at this point. (Open source)

The delivery of the J-7 to North Korea was preceded by a visit by leader Kim Il Sung to China and a visit to the aircraft factory in Chengdu. The model in the display case corresponds almost exactly to the J-7I version that North Korea then received. (KCNA)

In Chengdu, Kim Il Sung was also shown the then-current production model, the J-7II, as the cockpit roof frame in the foreground clearly belongs to this version. However, the fact that North Korea received the predecessor version, the J-7I – possibly in the form of used aircraft – could be due to the fact that the aircraft were provided to North Korea free of charge. (KCNA)

As photos from the era of the current leader Kim Jong Un show, the J-7Is, which have serials in the 700 range (image sources show numbers between 702 and 737), are still in service. Like all North Korean fighter aircraft, they have probably flown very few hours since entering service and are in a good condition. As with other types, the aircraft have evidently been equipped with a modern GR-400 radio from the Malaysian manufacturer Glocom with frequency hopping capability during overhaul. An indicator of this is GA-411B antenna from same manufacturer on the right below the cockpit.

As, regardless of the country's economic situation, in North Korea there is always sufficient material and human resources available (the KPAAF was said to have up to 70 airfields and 70,000 personnel) for the military, it could be assumed that the J-7I will remain in service for a long time to come, especially as there is no information about possible losses. The J-7s are flown by the 72nd Aviation Regiment of the 2nd Aviation Division, which is based at the Hwangsuwon Air Base in the north-east of the country.

Unfortunately, the resolution of this photo is not sufficient to identify the serial number on the landing gear cover on the left edge of the image. However, the '7' at the beginning clearly indicates a J-7. (Open source)

Preparation for night flight operations of J-7I. The fact that both pitot tubes and cone covers are attached to the aircraft in the background suggests – as with almost all images from North Korea – that this is a propaganda shot and that the aircraft are not about to take-off, as the image suggests. (Open source)

This propaganda photograph from more recent times shows the good maintenance condition of the J-7I, which is now quite old. The hopeless technical inferiority of the aircraft compared to those of the South Korean and US air forces on the other side of the demarcation line is obviously intended to be compensated for by ideologically strengthening the pilots. (Open source)

A photo of a J-7I with the current leader Kim Jong Un, indicating that this version is still in service today. The white antenna under the fuselage for the retrofitted GR-400 radio from Malaysian manufacturer Glocom is clearly visible. (KCNA)

8

MYANMAR

The former Burma gained independence from Great Britain in 1948 and was renamed Myanmar in 1989. Situated between India, China, Laos and Thailand, the agricultural country has a wide range of natural resources, which it is barely able to exploit. Since the end of the 1950s, military governments have repeatedly come to power. A civil war has been raging in the country for a long time and has flared up again since a coup d'état on 1 February 2021.

After its foundation, the Myanmar Air Force (*Tatmadaw Lay*) was equipped with British and later also US aircraft types. With the military coup of 1962 and the proclamation of the Socialist Republic of the Union of Burma, Eastern technology was added, while Western types continue to be procured.

Since another coup in 1988, Myanmar has a close military relationship with China, but also procures weapons systems from Russia. In the 1990s China delivered transport and training aircraft and finally F-7s to the Myanmar Air Force, possibly as free military aid. The first 10 F-7IIK single-seaters (serials 1601–1610) and two FT-7BK trainers (1611 and 1612) arrived at the Hmawbi Air Base near the capital Rangoon in May 1991. A further 48 F-7BKs (1613–1637, 1639–1641, 1643–1662, the existence of a possible 49th aircraft with the number 1642 is unconfirmed) and four FT-7BKs (1638, 1663–1665) followed by 1999. The deliveries also included 350 PL-2A AAMs and a batch of the more modern PL-5.

It has been reported several times that Israeli company Elbit had received an order to modernise the Myanmar F-7s – not least due to the aircraft's limited operational capabilities with Chinese avionics and their low reliability. Upgrades were said to have included equipping the aircraft with the Elta EL/M-2032 radar, the Rafael Python 3 AAM and the Rafael Litening laser targeting pod. However, none of these components has been seen on a Myanmar F-7. Instead, in the meantime Myanmar has procured new types with modern avionics: MiG-29, JF-17 and most recently FTC-2000G. It can therefore be assumed that the F-7s will remain in service with the Myanmar Air Force in their current configuration for the foreseeable future.

The aircraft are operated by 1 Squadron in Taungoo and 41 Squadron in Magway to the south and west of the capital Naypyidaw respectively, as well as by 4 Squadron in Nampong in the north of the country. At least six F-7IIK/BKs have been lost over the years, including unknown aircraft on 1 October 2002 and 22 January 2010,

1648 on 3 April 2018 and, in two independent accidents on 16 October 2018, 1640 and another unknown serial. Another F-7 crashed into a village not far from Mandalay on 10 June 2025, possibly having been shot down. Two aircraft (1623 and 1633) are on display at the Myanmar Defence Services Museum in the capital Naypyidaw.

At the end of 2022, Myanmar received six FTC-2000Gs from China, which were assigned the serials 1401–1406. The aircraft are flown by an as yet unknown squadron in Namsang, north-west of Naypyidaw. Six further aircraft in the serial range 1407–1413 (so there is either a gap in the allocation of numbers or there are actually as many as seven aircraft) entered service with *Tatmadaw Lay* in December 2024.

Various rebel armies, such as the Karen National Liberation Army (KNLA), the Karenni Nationalities Defence Force (KNDF) and the Kachin Independence Army (KIA), have been fighting against the ruling military junta in the civil war that has been raging since the beginning of 2021. They have been able to conquer large areas on the borders with Bangladesh, Thailand and China, while the military government controls the centre of the country. F-7s and especially FTC-2000s regularly fly missions in the fight against the insurgents. As the rebels possess an air defence thanks to foreign support, they have been able to inflict some losses on the government air force.

At least two FTC-2000Gs have been lost in the meantime; 1405 on 16 January 2024, and 1409 on 3 July 2025. The first aircraft was shot down by KIA rebels with a KN-6 MANPAD; the KNDF claims to have destroyed the second.

A Myanmar pilot with the rank of captain poses in front of his F-7BK. The pilot's helmet and anti-G pants are of Chinese origin. The blurred image of the missile under the wing makes it impossible to identify it clearly. It could be either a variant of the PL-2 or the PL-5. (Open source)

Myanmar F-7IIK on approach to Yangon. The aircraft carries a 720-litre drop-tank on the fuselage hardpoint and HF-7 rocket pods on the inner wing pylons. (Alexander Golz)

Of the total of six FT-7BKs, only a few pictures exist. 1638 belongs to the second delivery batch from the mid-1990s. The large areas of paint flaking at the rear are striking and may indicate inadequate priming, but also ongoing thermal problems. (Marc van Zon)

Next to the MiG-29s of the local 43 Squadron F-7IIKs, probably seconded from 1 Squadron in Taungoo, are parked under the shelters at Yangon International Airport. (Alexander Golz)

The procurement of newer models such as the MiG-29, JF-17 and FTC-2000G made it possible to retire older F-7BKs. This aircraft is part of the extensive collection at the Defence Services Museum in Myanmar's capital Naypyidaw. (Guido E. Bühlmann)

One of the six FTC-2000Gs from the second batch delivered in December 2024, sporting the eye-catching factory paint job. (Open source)

From this angle, the extremely large chaff and flare dispensers under the rear fuselage are striking. On the FT-7 and the classic FTC-2000, these were located between the two fins under the tail. (Open source)

A KIA fighter poses in front of the wreckage of the FTC-2000G 1405, which was shot down by this rebel movement on 16 January 2024. (Open source)

9

NAMIBIA

The former German South West Africa had been under South African administration since 1918. From the mid-sixties, SWAPO (the South West Africa People's Organisation) fought against the South Africans. In 1989, elections were held in the country under UN supervision, as a result of which the country gained its independence in 1990.

With the help of foreign support, including from the USA, India, Libya and China, Namibia began to build up its own air force in 1994, initially as part of the army. The initial equipment was a colourful mix of US Cessna O-2As, Indian Cheetah and Chetak helicopters, Chinese Y-12 transport aircraft and Mi-8/24s from Libya. Even an An-26 of the former East German Air Force, found its way to southern Africa. It was not until 13 March 2005 that the Namibian Air Force was formed as an independent branch of the armed forces with a ceremony at Grootfontein base, with the official founding date being 23 June 2002. Shortly after this, at the end of 2004, Namibia ordered F-7s from China to equip the new force. In addition, four K-8 jet trainers and two Y-9 transport aircraft were procured. Namibian personnel went to China for training.

In February 2005, the first of six F-7NMs arrived in Namibia and were assembled by Chinese technicians. After the pilots had completed their retraining, the F-7s were officially put into service on the occasion of Independence Day on 23 June 2006. The single-seaters were given the serials 0310, 0313, 0315, 0317, 0319 and 0321. In October 2006, the fleet was completed by two two-seater FT-7NMs with the serials 0330 and 0331. The aircraft, which belong to 23 Fighter Squadron, are based at Grootfontein Air Base in the north of the country, which was originally built by South Africa.

The F-7NM with serial 0315 was destroyed in a landing accident at Ondangwa airfield on 15 October 2021. The other aircraft are likely to remain the backbone of the Namibian Air Force for the foreseeable future.

On both of these F-7NMs, the outer wing pylons for the drop-tanks are fitted, but not the inner ones for armament. The two 30mm cannons, one on either side of the lower fuselage, are also clearly visible. (Open source)

An F-7NM taking-off during an airshow in Windhoek in 2015. Like all other export versions, the Namibian aircraft have a unique colour scheme that cannot be found in any other user country. (Open source)

10

NIGERIA

After 100 years of British colonial rule, Nigeria was granted independence in 1960. Separatist movements in various regions and numerous military coups have repeatedly destabilised the Federal Republic of Nigeria and its 36 states. Although the populous and oil-rich country never steered a socialist course, a total of 25 MiG-21MFs and six MiG-21UM twin-seaters were procured from the USSR for the Nigerian Air Force (NAF) in 1975, after MiG-17s had already flown in Nigerian service. Due to relatively high attrition, a delivery of MiG-21bis followed in 1984. However, these only remained in service for around a decade before the lack of spare parts and other resources permanently grounded them. Reports of a reactivation of the MiG-21 fleet or its modernisation by RAC MiG or Israel Aircraft Industries proved to be false. In the meantime, surveillance of Nigerian airspace was exclusively in the hands of jet trainers such as the L-39 and Alpha Jet.

In September 2005, Nigeria signed a contract for the delivery of 15 Chinese F-7s for more than US$220 million. These were 12 F-7NI single-seaters (NAF800–NAF811) and three FT-7NI trainers (NAF812–NAF814). Nigeria ordered PL-9C AAMs, unguided rockets and bombs for a further US$32 million. The aircraft were delivered by sea in early 2010. Before, 12 Nigerian pilots and a number of technicians had been sent to China for training. The technical personnel underwent a three-month training programme at the manufacturer's plant in Chengdu, while the pilots remained in China for even longer. In the meantime, Chengdu factory representatives had assembled and test-flown three FT-7NI two-seaters at the 64 Air Defence Group site in Makurdi. Two of the aircraft were presented at the NAF Air Expo 2010 in the static and flight display, respectively, flown by mixed Nigerian-Chinese crews. Afterwards, F-7NI single-seaters were commissioned.

However, the fleet suffered early losses. On 22 March 2011, an F-7NI (presumably NAF803) crashed in Kano, killing the pilot. Two months later, on 11 May 2011, an FT-7NI (NAF813) was involved in an accident, but the crew managed to eject. Subsequently, the F-7s experienced intensive missions against the Islamist terrorist organisation Boko Haram. On 10 October 2015, the loss of another F-7NI (possibly NAF801) was reported. An F-7 and an FT-7 collided during training for the Independence Day celebrations on 28 September 2018, FT-7NI NAF812 was lost and the second aircraft suffered damage. One pilot was killed. On 14 July 2023, FT-7NI NAF814 had an accident during a training flight over the home base in Makurdi. Both crew members were able to eject, but now there were no two-seater aircraft available for flight training.

The ceremonial commissioning of the Nigerian FT-7 (and other types) took place at the NAF Air Expo 2010 in Kaduna. Here, Nigerian President Goodluck Jonathan, who had just taken office, inspects one of the two-seaters on display at the event. (Holger Müller)

This J-7I of the Korean People's Army Air Force is shown in livery as delivered: this consisted of two layers of clear lacquer, mixed with 10 percent and 5 percent aluminium powder, respectively, and was known as 'silver-grey' amongst ground crews. As such, the jet was still lacking the antenna for a modern radio system under the fuselage, installed more recently. In addition to two internal 30mm cannon, the primary armament consisted of PL-2 infrared-homing, short-range air-to-air missiles. Arguably, these were never shown actually installed on any North Korean J-7s. (Artwork by Tom Cooper)

In 1990, Sri Lanka placed an order for four F-7BS interceptors. This sub-variant represented an improved F-7B, with features of the J-7II and the F-7M: powered by the WP-7B engine, it had four underwing hardpoints, improved air conditioning for the cockpit and avionics bay, and was delivered together with PL-5 air-to-air missiles, as illustrated here. Delivered in white overall, the F-7BS were soon repainted in mid-grey overall, and received serial numbers CF704, CF705, CF707, and CF708. While No. 5 Squadron was officially established at Katunayake AB on 1 February 1991, conversion training was conducted with the help of Chinese instructors on two FT-5s (CTF701 and CTF702), and, later on, on a single FT-7BS (CTF703). (Artwork by Tom Cooper)

Seeking to counter the LTTE's growing air wing, in 2007 Sri Lanka ordered four F-7GS, compatible with PL-5 air-to-air missiles and a wide range of air-to-ground weaponry. Still assigned to No. 5 Squadron, and wearing a camouflage pattern in two greys, as shown here, for the rest of the war in Sri Lanka, the jets wore serial numbers CF780, CF781, CF782 and CF783: subsequently, they were reserialled as SFI5104, SFI5105, SFI5106, and SFI5108, respectively. On 9 September 2008, one of them was used to shoot down an LTTE-operated Zlin-142 as it was underway at an altitude of less than 500 metres. (Artwork by Tom Cooper)

Pakistan became not only the largest, but also the export customer most influential for further development of the F-7, and even for its export success. The Pakistan Air Force prompted the Chinese into development of two early advanced versions – the F-7MP and F-7P – both custom-tailored to Pakistani requirements. The first resulting contract (Handshake-I) stipulated the delivery of 20 F-7MPs (and four FT-7Bs). Delivered between June and November 1988, and wearing serials 88-501 to 88-520, they entered service with No. 20 Squadron, and were not only equipped with such Western equipment as Martin Baker ejection seats, but compatible with US-made weaponry, like AIM-9N/P Sidewinder missiles, as illustrated here. The large splotch of grey colour applied under the cockpit was used to cover the inscription 'Airguard' – a name the PAF did not officially adopt. (Artwork by Tom Cooper)

Hard on the heels of acquiring the first 20 F-7MPs within Project Handshake-I, the PAF followed-up with Project Handshake-II, comprising an order for 40 improved F-7Ps. Receiving serials 89-521 to 89-560, these were delivered between 1989 and 1993, and eventually served with Nos. 18, 19, and 2 Squadrons. Outwardly, they showed next to no difference to F-7MPs: the camouflage pattern, armament and equipment (like drop tanks, shown here in bare metal overall, as used early during their service) remained the same and no unit insignia was applied. (Artwork by Tom Cooper)

The second batch of F-7Ps from Project Handshake-II comprised jets with serials in the range 90-561 to 90-580. They retained the same camouflage patterns but soon after service entry began receiving unit insignia on their fins. Starting in 2001, all the surviving F-7MPs and F-7Ps were reequipped with FIAR Grifo pulse Doppler radars while undergoing overhauls at Kamra. (Artwork by Tom Cooper)

The need for the development of a two-seat conversion trainer for the J-7/F-7 family became obvious almost as soon as the exports of these began: to bridge the gap, the Chinese had to temporarily lease older and slower FT-5s to customers like Zimbabwe and Sri Lanka. Meanwhile, the process of developing the FT-7 led to the emergence of the FT-7B, the first four of which – serial numbers 88-601 to 88-604 – were delivered to Pakistan in 1988. They differed from all subsequent aircraft in a camouflage pattern in dark stone, light earth, and black-green on top surfaces and sides, and light blue on undersides. (Artwork by Tom Cooper)

The FT-7Ps delivered under Project Handshake-III, were the first with a stretched fuselage and the Chinese double-barrelled 23-3 gun (installed low on the centre fuselage), and also the first to receive the same avionics outfit and camouflage pattern as the F-7MP and F-7P single-seaters. Deployed for advanced jet- and tactical training, they were frequently sighted while carrying drop tanks on outboard underwing pylons and AIM-9N/P Sidewinder air-to-air missiles. (Artwork by Tom Cooper)

The latest version of the two-seat conversion trainer acquired by Pakistan became the FT-7PG, nine of which were acquired by Pakistan in 2001 and 2002. They retained the original delta-shaped wing. Their serial numbers were 02-681 to 02-687, and 03-688 to 03-689. While wearing the standardised camouflage pattern introduced with F-7MPs and F-7Ps, nowadays, the surviving jets of this sub-variant are frequently decorated with large inscriptions denoting the nicknames of squadrons operating them, in this case, 'Cheetahs' of No. 20 Air Superiority Squadron, established in 1956 and presently home-based at the PAF Base Mauripur (better known as 'Masroor'), outside Karachi. As of the early 2020s, their principal air-to-air armament comprised AIM-9M Sidewinder missiles. (Artwork by Tom Cooper)

Following extensive evaluation of the F-7MG with double delta wing and improved avionics, in 1997 Pakistan placed an order for 48 F-7PGs. Delivered in 2001–2002, these were originally painted in something like a Chinese version of the standardised PAF camouflage pattern (introduced with deliveries of US-made F-16s in the mid-1980s) – in which the dark sea grey colour covered all of the rear fuselage and the wing. F-7PGs received serial numbers 01-801 to 01-820, and 02-821 to 02-848 and, amongst others, served with the Combat Command School of the PAF, home-based at the Sargodha complex. Their primary armament comprised AIM-9M Sidewinder air-to-air missiles. (Artwork by Tom Cooper)

Photographed before receiving the unit insignia on its fin, this F-7PG belonged to the final batch of this type delivered to Pakistan in 2002. While the first batch of this variant was assigned to No. 17 Squadron, the second went to No. 23 Squadron (both were home-based at Samungli AB, outside Quetta), replacing the obsolete Shenyang F-6s. The balance from a total of 48 F-7PGs was assigned to the Combat Command School at Sargodha and No. 20 Squadron at Rafiqui Air Base, where they replaced remaining F-7Ps. (Artwork by Tom Cooper)

In the course of their overhauls in Pakistan, the F-7PGs were gradually reequipped with advanced FIAR Grifo pulse Doppler radars and repainted in the standardised camouflage pattern reminiscent of the earlier F-16s and F-7Ps. As in the case of FT-7s, all presently wear the insignia of the squadrons flying them: the example illustrated here was operated by No. 17 'Tigers' Squadron. Their armament remained almost entirely of US design, including AIM-9M Sidewinders and the Mk.80-series general purpose bombs: with Chinese support, the PAF has meanwhile developed a number of kits enabling their conversion to GPS-assisted glide bombs. (Artworks by Tom Cooper)

After operating a mix of Chinese-made F-6s and A-5s, Soviet/Russian-made MiG-29s, and US-made Northrop F-5E/F Tiger IIs for decades, in 2015, Sudan opted for six FTC-2000s. Delivered starting in 2017, these received a unique camouflage pattern consisting of light stone, dark earth and dark green on upper surfaces and sides, and light blue on undersides. Their serials were in the range 1201 to 1206. During operations prior to the civil war that erupted in 2023, they were mostly seen equipped with drop tanks on outboard underwing hardpoints, and Chinese-made HF-7 pods for unguided rockets on inboard pylons. (Artwork by Tom Cooper)

At the outbreak of the latest civil war in Sudan, in April 2023 the Rapid Support Forces (RSF) launched multiple attacks on the bases of the Sudanese Air Force. Amongst others, they overran Merowe airport north of Khartoum, capturing at least four FTC-2000s, damaging one and destroying another. Once the RSF was forced to abandon this facility, the Sudanese rushed to recover the aircraft and return them to service, and they flew dozens of air strikes. Although Sudan acquired PL-9C air-to-air missiles for their FTC-2000s, the survivors are primarily deployed for ground attack purposes, still armed with HF-7 pods. (Artwork by Tom Cooper)

Tanzania placed an order for 12 F-7TN single-seaters in 2009 and received them two years later. They became the only single-seaters of the final generation to wear a single-colour camouflage livery in mid-grey overall. All received service titles (TAFC) and their four-digit serials (with prefix JW, for the Tanzanian Defence Force) – though applied in a rather unusual fashion. While the title TAFC is stencilled on the left front side of the fuselage, it is the serial – in this case JW 9243 – which is applied on the opposite side. Roundels – comprising the crest of Tanzania – were applied in six positions. (Artwork by Tom Cooper)

Unlike the F-7TNs, Tanzanian FT-7TNs were camouflaged in light stone, light green and dark brown-green, applied following a standardised camouflage pattern introduced a few years earlier. The example here – one of two delivered in 2011 (serial numbers JW9242 and JW9253) – is shown as marked on delivery, including the full crest of the Tanzanian Defence Forces on the fin, and the serial on the forward fuselage. (Artwork by Tom Cooper)

The F-7s of the Air Force of Zimbabwe (AFZ) went through a particularly interesting transformation over time. The country received a total of 12 single-seaters, the first four (serials 700–703) of which had only one hardpoint per wing, and all of which were painted in matt white overall. Their original armament comprised PL-2 air-to-air missiles (shown as insets in the lower right corner): these were replaced by PL-5s in the late 1990s (lower left corner). Furthermore, the 'Zimbabwe Bird' originally served as the fin-flash, before being replaced in the mid-1990s. (Artworks by Tom Cooper)

In the mid-1980s, the Zimbabwe Bird (or 'Zimbabwean Pidgeon') was replaced by the flag of Zimbabwe. Moreover, during an overhaul in 1998–1999, the surviving jets received an upgrade including a modern instrument landing system, a new communication suite, and an entirely new, wrap-around camouflage pattern, including dark grey in addition to matt white. Around the same time, the AFZ is said to have begun acquiring additional weaponry and making this compatible with its F-7s. Supposedly, included were not only UB-32-57 pods of Soviet/Russian origin – shown here installed on underwing hardpoints – but also – shown underneath the main artwork – French-made Matra F4 pods for unguided 68mm rockets; UB-16-57 pods; and Chinese-made PL-7 air-to-air missiles. However, no photographic evidence of these conversions could be found so far. (Artworks by Tom Cooper)

In 1999–2001, No. 7 Squadron AFZ was commanded by Squadron Leader Michael Enslin, a veteran Hawk pilot of the Second Congo War. During his tour of duty, Enslin had the freshly overhauled jet with serial number 711 marked with his personal insignia. Around the same time, the Zimbabwean F-7s are said to be made compatible with Soviet/Russian-made R-60MK infrared-homing, short-range air-to-air missiles. This resulted in them becoming capable of being deployed in a wide range of configurations, including the one shown here: a pair of R-60MKs on the P-62-2M dual launch rail on the outboard underwing pylon, and a single PL-7 on the inboard underwing pylon. Notable is the 720-litre drop tank installed under the centreline. Again, there is no photographic evidence of the conversions shown here available. (Artwork by Tom Cooper)

The two Zimbabwean FT-7s (serial numbers 730 and 731) underwent a similar transformation over time. Since their overhauls in 1999–2001, they also wear the same camouflage pattern as the single-seaters. Allegedly, they were made compatible with a wide range of weaponry acquired from abroad, including APU-68 launch rails for S-24 heavy 240mm unguided rockets (not shown here). (Artworks by Tom Cooper)

The F-7Bs acquired by the USA for the 4477th Test and Evaluation Squadron (also known as the 'Red Eagles') were painted in a wide range of very different liveries. Some received an overall light grey colour, one or two were painted in white overall, but most received disruptive camouflage patterns in grey and green. This example is one of the few where enough photographs are available to reconstruct the pattern as applied on the left side of the jet: this was applied in tan (probably FS33531, similar to mid stone), light brown (FS30450), and dark earth (FS20095 or 30140). In addition to a two-digit 'bort' number on the forward fuselage, this jet had a 'fake' national insignia consisting of the Red Star outlined in yellow (on Soviet aircraft, the Red Star was always outlined in white). As far as is known, F-7Bs of the USAF wore no maintenance stencils, but many had pilot names applied under the left side of the cockpit. (Artwork by Tom Cooper)

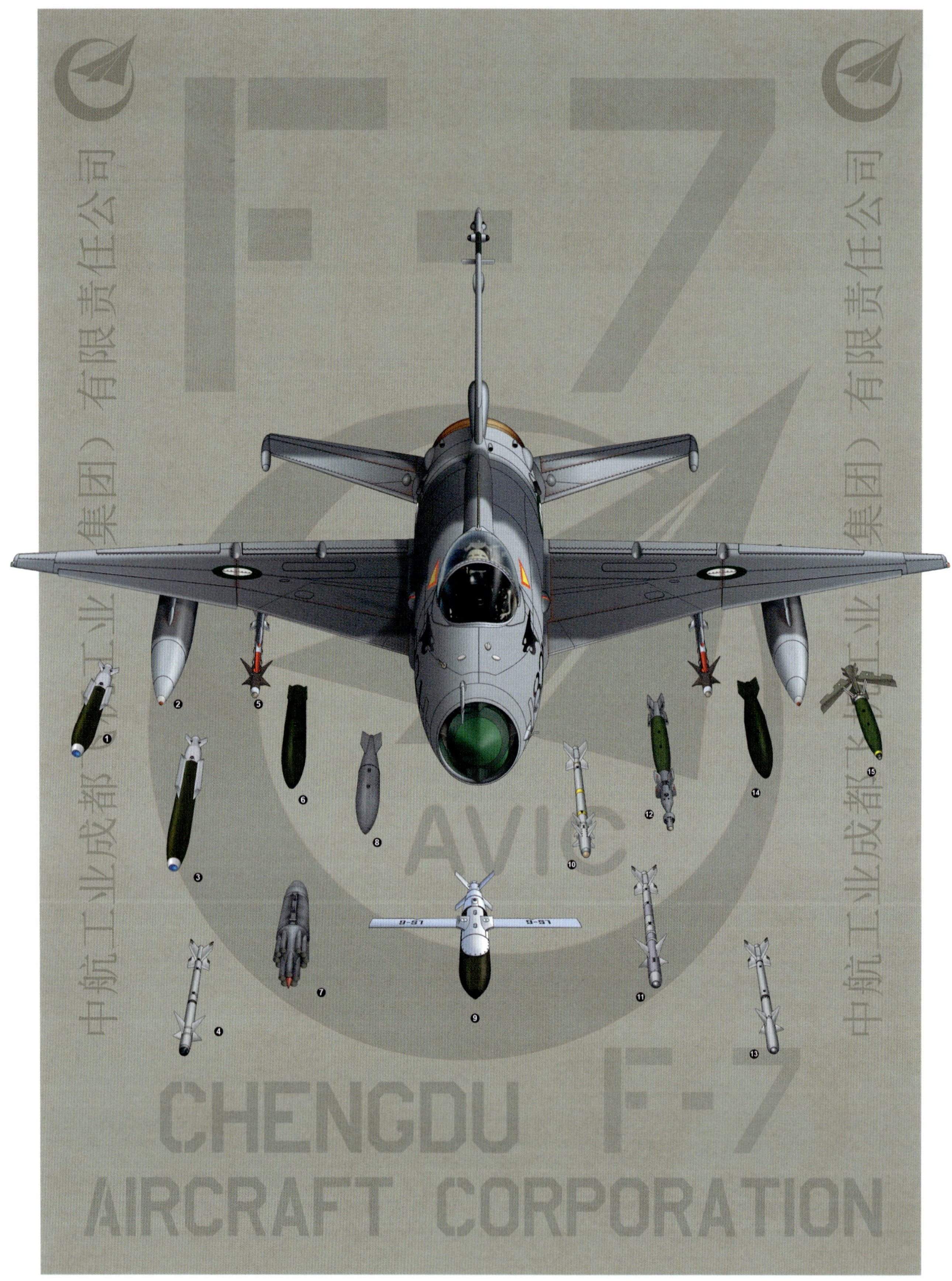

The aircraft shown is an F-7PG, serial 02-821 from No. 17 'Tigers' Squadron, PAF (see colour profile at the bottom of page iv), and here represents exported F-7s and their armament as used by a variety of clients. The inscription in Mandarin reads: Aviation Industry Corporation of China Ltd., AVIC.

1: LS-6 50kg satellite-guided bomb (BAF); 2: 490-litre drop tank; 3: LS-6 100kg satellite-guided bomb (BAF); 4: PL-2 air-to-air missile (AFZ); 5: AIM-9M air-to-air missile (PAF); 6: NORINCO Type-250-3 low-drag general-purpose bomb, parachute-retarded variant (all customers); 7: UB-16-57 rocket pod (representative of various pods of Chinese origin); 8: NORINCO Type-250-3 low-drag anti-personnel bomb (PAF, SLAF, AFZ); 9: LS-6 250kg satellite-guided bomb (BAF and PAF); 10: PL-7 air-to-air missile; 11: PL-9 air-to-air missile; 12: GBU-12 Paveway II 250kg laser-guided bomb (PAF); 13: PL-5 air-to-air missile; 14: NORINCO Type-250 general-purpose bomb (PAF & SLAF); 15: Mk.82 with Mk.12 Snakeye retarding fins (PAF & SLAF); (Artwork by Anderson Subtil)

A Nigerian pilot in front of his F-7NI. The smoke marks on the muzzle of the left gun indicate that the weapon was recently fired. (DefenceNigeria)

Preparations for take-off on an F-7NI. The aircraft is armed with Chinese low-drag 250kg bombs. (NAF)

Although the NAF has since procured the JF-17 as a potential successor, the F-7 remains the most important fighter aircraft in its arsenal in terms of numbers, but the number of operational aircraft had declined rapidly. In November 2020, the Chief of Air Staff of the Nigerian Air Force therefore announced the reactivation of nine F-7s (though it is not clear whether this figure also included the remaining two-seater at this time). Seven of the aircraft had to be brought to China for industrial overhaul, while only two could be overhauled locally with Chinese support. In October 2022, all nine aircraft were back from overhaul and were supplemented by a 10th, another two-seater FT-7NI (NAF815), which China was supposedly providing free of charge. The only operator of the F/FT-7NI is today's 101st Air Defence Group in Makurdi.

Brake chute landing of an F-7NI in Yola. With a runway length of 3,000 metres available there, the use of the chute is actually unnecessary. (PRNigeria)

Initially, the Nigerian two-seaters flew without wing pylons. These were added later. From this perspective, the chaff and flare dispenser between the fins under the tail is clearly visible. (Holger Müller)

The FT-7NI NAF813 landing in Kaduna. The camouflage pattern of the Nigerian F/FT-7 with two shades of green and one shade of brown is just as unique as that of the other users. The aircraft shown crashed on 11 May 2011. (Holger Müller)

Pre-flight checks at FT-7NI NAF813. A Nigerian pilot sits in the front cockpit, with a Chinese instructor in the back seat. The ground crew is also supervised by a Chinese instructor (not visible). (Holger Müller)

11

PAKISTAN

The state of Pakistan was created in 1947 from the predominantly Muslim parts of British India, while the areas with a Hindu or other majority population and most of the predominantly Muslim Kashmir were absorbed into present-day India. Arbitrary border demarcations by the colonial power, which disregarded demographic conditions, were the cause of a conflict between the two neighbours that has been smouldering since the state was founded and has had a major impact on Pakistan's development.

The US arms embargo following the 1965 Indo-Pakistani war forced the Pakistan Air Force (PAF, Pakistan *Fiza'ya*), which was largely US-equipped at the time, to look for alternative suppliers. As the USSR and Great Britain traditionally supported India, only France and above all China remained. After deliveries of large numbers of FT-5 (MiG-17 twin-seater), F-6 (MiG-19) and A-5 (heavily modified fighter-bomber version of the MiG-19) in the mid-1960s, it was only logical that Pakistan also added the successor model F-7 to its inventory.

While the PAF received a total of 40 F-16s from the USA by 1986, at the same time it intensively supported China in the development of the F-7M and initiated the development of the F-7MP and F-7P versions tailored to Pakistani requirements. The reasons for this may have been the 'freezing' of an initial contract for the delivery of F-16s by the US Congress shortly beforehand and the not unfounded fear of a repetition as well as the high operating costs of the US type.

The first batch, 'Handshake-I', of 20 F-7MPs and four FT-7Bs arrived at No. 20 Squadron in Shorkot (Rafiqui) between June and November 1988. The single-seaters were given the serials 88-501–88-520, the twin-seaters 88-601–88-604. Shortly before, in May of the same year, the PAF sent seven pilots to China for retraining. Under the designation 'Handshake-II', a further 60 F-7Ps were delivered to No. 18 and 19 squadrons in Rafiqui and Sargodha (Mushaf) – both of which were later transferred to Mianwali as retraining units (OCU) – and to No. 2 Squadron in Masroor in 1989–90. Aircraft from this delivery got the serials 89-521–89-560 and 90-561–90-580, followed by 15 two-seater FT-7Ps in three batches (eight, three and four aircraft) as 'Handshake-III' in 1991–92, the first of which was delivered to No. 19 (OCU) Squadron. These aircraft were assigned the serial ranges 90-605–90-615 and 92-616–92-619 (according to other sources, there were only 14 aircraft with 92-618 as the highest serial). After the arrival of the FT-7P, the FT-7Bs, which only served as a temporary solution, were returned to China. The final delivery of up to 40 additional F-7Ps was made in 1993 as 'Handshake-IV' to

Three F-7MPs and one FT-7B immediately after their transfer from China to Pakistan. Clearly visible are the aircraft's original equipment with the Chinese HTY-2 ejection seat and the paint marks under the cockpit, which were used to cover up the 'Skybolt' designation rejected by the PAF. (Open source)

An F-7MP dropping its brake chute upon landing. The aircraft is 'armed' with two Sidewinder training missiles. Here, the antennas of the RWR are located on a bulge of the vertical stabiliser, while the following F-7P carries these antennas on its upper edge. (Open source)

the Combat Commanders' School in Sarghoda and No. 14 Squadron in Kamra (Minhas) and comprised serials 93-701 to (allegedly) 93-740; the highest number that can currently be verified is 93-731. The deliveries of the 1990s were completed by five FT-7P two-seaters, which were given the serials 93-653–93-657 (according to other sources, six aircraft, starting with 93-652).

Since the original equipment of the F-7P with the GEC-Marconi Skyranger 7M radar rangefinder considerably reduced the combat value of the aircraft, a call for tenders for a cost-effective yet powerful radar was issued in the mid-1990s. The Italian FIAR with its Grifo emerged as the winner of the competition and in June 1993 a contract was signed for the licence production of about 100 of these devices at the Kamra Avionics, Electronics and Radar Factory (KARF), where their industrial overhaul still takes place today. However, production of the Grifo in Kamra did not start until 2001. Within three years, all F-7Ps received the new radar.

After an embargo imposed between 1990 and 2005 due to Pakistan's nuclear weapons programme prevented the delivery of F-16s already ordered from the USA and consequently no modern Western fighter aircraft were available, the PAF began evaluating the F-7MG with double-delta wing and improved avionics in 1997. The trials were successful and 48 F-7PGs and nine FT-7PGs were ordered for delivery in 2001 and 2002. The single-seaters got the serials 01.801–01.820 and 02.821–02.848, the twin-seaters the serials 02.681–02.687 as well as 03.688 and 03.689. The procurement was again preceded by training of Pakistani personnel in China. Around 100 PAF pilots and technicians were sent there in 2001.

Three F-7MPs in flight shortly after entering service. While the front and rear aircraft carry Sidewinder missiles, the centre aircraft carries a PL-7. (Open source)

Two of the four FT-7Bs delivered to Pakistan on loan are seen here during a training flight. The aircraft of this version were the only ones in Pakistani service to fly with green and brown camouflage. All other aircraft are painted in various shades of grey. (Open Source)

Maintenance work on an F-7P. The aircraft belongs to the second delivery batch Handshake-II. (Holger Müller)

Pre-flight checks at flightline in Mianwali. At the time the photo was taken in 2004, there were only a few roofed areas available for aircraft. Since then, the infrastructure on site has been massively expanded. (Holger Müller)

Armed with Sidewinder missiles, an F-7P flies over a radar site in the mountains of Pakistan. (PAF)

An F-7P with two drop-tanks and empty Sidewinder launch rails taxies to take-off. The traces of smoke on the muzzle of the left cannon indicated that the weapon was recently fired. The yellowish, as yet unpainted, sheet metal on the vertical stabiliser with a clearly visible bulge is striking. This was not yet present upon delivery and suggests that a previously unknown component has been retrofitted. (Holger Müller)

An engine test is being prepared on an FT-7P from last delivery batch of the 1990s. Since not only the tail section has been removed, but the ejection seats are also missing, the technicians have to sit on makeshift seats during these tests. (Holger Müller)

The first batch of 20 F-7PGs was airfreighted to Karachi in late 2001 and assembled at the nearby Masroor base. No. 17 Squadron at the Samungli base near Quetta received these aircraft, where they made their first flights in January 2002 and finally replaced the F-6s in March of the same year. No. 23 Squadron, also at Samungli, was equipped with a further 20 F-7PGs. The rest of the aircraft went to No. 20 Squadron in Rafiqui, where they replaced the F-7P. At the end of 2002 through to the beginning of 2003, No. 17 Squadron, which acted as the training unit for the new version, received the nine FT-7PGs ordered. The F/FT-7PGs were delivered without a radar. Retrofit of the advanced Grifo PG took place in Pakistan.

With Pakistan once again enjoying the favour of the USA, the decision was taken in 2006 to procure new F-16s and upgrade the existing ones. But due to the mixed experiences from the cooperation with the West, the PAF turned to China for the large-scale modernisation of its fleet. In return, China responded to the requirements of its most important export customer. The result of this close cooperation is the JF-17 Thunder, specially developed for Pakistan, which today forms the backbone of the PAF and is produced in workshare between Chengdu and Kamra since the beginning of 2008. More than 100 JF-17s are now in service and have already superseded the F-7P in almost all frontline units. Further JF-17s are to replace the remaining F-7PGs, although it can be assumed that they will continue in the training role, together with the FT-7P and FT-7PG. Arguments in favour of this are the maintenance capability available in the country and the comparatively low operating costs.

Take-off of an FT-7P, equipped with two drop-tanks, in Mianwali. This picture, which was available for some time in high resolution at author's website www.mig-21.de, found its way from there through the Internet and into various publications – always without citing the source. Even Martin-Baker company used this image (with a strangely bent pitot tube) on its social media channels without naming the author. (Holger Müller)

Maintenance of F-7P and FT-5 in Mianwali in the open air. The smoke marks on the fuselage of the F-7P indicate that the cannon was fired recently. (Holger Müller)

According to the squadron insignia on the vertical stabiliser, this landing FT-7P belongs to No. 19 (Operation Conversion Unit, OCU) Squadron, based in Mianwali at the time the photo was taken. This unit now flies F-16s from Bholari, while F/FT-7s in Mianwali are still operated by No. 20 (OCU) and Shooter (LIFT) Squadron. (Holger Müller)

Two F-7PGs over the snowy peaks of the Himalayas. The aircraft in the foreground belongs to No. 23 Air Superiority Squadron *Talons* in Samungli, the one behind it, whose squadron emblem is largely obscured, probably to No. 17 Air Superiority Squadron *Tigers* in Peshawar. Despite Chinese advances in AAMs, the PAF – as shown here – relied on American AIM-9 Sidewinders also for the most modern F-7 version in its inventory. (PAF)

F/FT-7PGs are still flying with No. 17 Air Superiority Squadron in Peshawar, No. 23 Combat Commanders School Squadron in Mushaf and No. 20 Operational Conversion (OCU) Squadron in Mianwali. The Shooter (LIFT) Squadron at the same base, which was only established in December 2017, is the last remaining user of the F/FT-7P. Among former users of the F-7P was Combat Commanders' School F-7 Squadron in Sargodha, while No. 18 and No. 20 Operational Conversion squadrons in Mianwali occasionally operated a mix of F-7P, FT-7P, F-7PG and FT-7PG.

The F-7s are also flown by female pilots – quite remarkable in an Islamic country. Pakistan's F-7s never saw real combat and therefore never fought against Indian MiG-21s. There is also no evidence that the Pakistani F-7 fleet was affected by the Indian air strikes as part of 'Operation Sindoor' in May 2025 or was involved in the Pakistani counter-operation 'Bunyan-un-Marsoos'. Confirmed loss reports are available for a total of 25 aircraft, although information for the early operational period up to the year 2000 is rather sparse. In relation to the number of aircraft procured, it is primarily the two-seaters that were affected by the losses. At least seven of the 20 FT-7Ps and four of the nine FT-7PGs have been lost. Furthermore, at least four F-7P and 10 F-7PG have crashed. Table 1 gives a list of known accidents.

The industrial overhaul of the Pakistani F-7s is carried out locally, at Pakistan Aeronautical Complex (PAC) in Kamra, north-west of the capital Islamabad. The first F-7P overhauled there left the facility in January 1994, followed by FT-7Ps since 1996, F-7PGs since 2007 and FT-7PGs since 2008. The facility also overhauls aircraft and components from other countries, such as Sri Lanka and Bangladesh.

Table 1: Known Accidents Involving Pakistan Air Force F-7s

Version	Date	Serial and notes
F-7P	30 July 1998	89-540
F-7P	5 August 2009	
F-7P	11 July 2013	
F-7P	9 August 2017	
F-7PG	10 December 2002*	(Mid-air collision)
F-7PG	10 December 2002*	
F-7PG	8 February 2012	
F-7PG	29 May 2012	
F-7PG	1 October 2014	
F-7PG	9 September 2015	
F-7PG	24 September 2016	
F-7PG	25 May 2017	02-830
F-7PG	17 August 2017	01-808
F-7PG	23 January 2019	
FT-7P	6 February 1996	
FT-7P	22 October 1996	
FT-7P	29 May 2009	
FT-7P	15 August 2011	90-609
FT-7P	25 January 2012	
FT-7P	7 January 2020	90-611
FT-7P	25 May 2022	
FT-7PG	15 February 2007	02-681
FT-7PG	13 March 2007	
FT-7PG	24 November 2015	03-689
FT-7PG	26 June 2018	

An F-7PG during a multinational exercise in the United Arab Emirates in 2009. Clearly visible is the grey two-tone paint scheme which makes the already not very large aircraft look even smaller, and thus more difficult for the enemy to detect. (USAF/Staff Sgt. Michael B. Keller)

The same aircraft from a different angle. The aircraft is carrying three drop-tanks and a Sidewinder on the right inner wing pylon. The nose flaps are slightly extended for the low-speed approach to the photo platform. (USAF/Staff Sgt. Michael B. Keller)

During its service, the original grey two-tone camouflage of the F-7PG had been supplemented by various additional unit insignia. On their flypast on the occasion of Pakistan Day on 23 March 2021, these aircraft of No. 17 Air Superiority Squadron *Tigers* from Peshawar carry their squadron insignia on the vertical stabiliser and under the cockpit as well as checkerboard patterns on the nose and on the tips of the drop-tanks in addition to the squadron name. (Awais Lali)

Furthermore, there is an inscription on the left side below the cockpit 'Fly Past 23rd March 2021' and – so that no one could question the affiliation to the unit – a large 'Tigers' title on the fuselage. (Awais Lali)

F-7PG of the No. 23 Air Superiority Squadron *Talons* taking-off from their home base in Samungli, which also serves as the international airport for the neighbouring city of Quetta. (Awais Lali)

The FT-7PG combines the airframe of the FT-7P with the new equipment of the F-7PG, but still features the classic delta wing. The 03-688 pictured here was the penultimate F-7 delivered to the PAF. The picture taken in 2014 shows the aircraft of No. 17 Air Superiority Squadron *Tigers* at Quetta-Samungli Air Base, where the unit was based at that time as part of 31 Wing. (Alan Warnes)

12

SRI LANKA

In 1948, shortly after its large neighbour India, Sri Lanka gained its independence from Great Britain but remained a member of the Commonwealth. Since the mid-1970s, a bloody battle raged in the country between the government and the separatists of the Liberation Tigers of Tamil Eelam (LTTE), also known as the 'Tamil Tigers', who were fighting for an independent state for the Tamil ethnic group in the north and east of the island. From 1983, the clashes escalated into a full-scale war. In the course of the war, the Sri Lankan armed forces were massively expanded and rearmed – although the Sri Lanka Air Force (SLAF) not as much as the other two branches of the armed forces. Nevertheless, the air force received jet aircraft for the first time in more than a decade. When asked why an interceptor with at best a secondary air-to-ground role was being procured instead of a fighter-bomber with the F-7, the relevant sources provide different explanations. One version referred to the year 1987, when India intervened in this conflict and sought to enforce a peace agreement. In the course of Indian operations, transport aircraft from the neighbouring country, escorted by Mirage 2000s, operated without restriction in Sri Lankan airspace. In response, the expansion of the air force by an air defence component was intended to prevent a recurrence. The version wherein China, the only country prepared to supply fighter aircraft, categorically excluded was the sale of fighter-bombers such as the A-5 and only offered F-7s, seems more logical. In August 1990, a SLAF delegation travelled to Chengdu and ordered four single-seaters and one two-seater. As the SLAF had not had any operational experience of jet aircraft for years and the required pilots had to be trained from scratch, two FT-5s (two-seater MiG-17s) were also procured as advanced trainers.

On 1 February 1991, No. 5 Jet Squadron was set up at the Katunayake base near the capital Colombo for the deployment of these aircraft. The crews were trained by Chinese instructors, who were not allowed to instruct their students in air-to-ground missions in accordance with government regulations – a further argument in favour of the fact that the procurement of the F-7 was not a free decision by the SLAF. Three of the five Sri Lankan jet pilots then acquired the missing knowledge on a three-month course in Pakistan. In July 1991, the two FT-5s were delivered. The first flight of the F-7BS took place on 13 September 1991 and in the following month (according to other sources not before December) a total of four aircraft and one FT-7BS trainer were delivered to Sri Lanka. The F-7BS were given the serials CF704, CF705, CF707 and CF708, while the FT-7BS flew as CTF703.

An F-7BS in the delivery livery, which, however, already shows some signs of use. (Holger Müller Collection)

Not only the worn grey paintwork, but above all the MiG-23UB in the background indicate that this picture was taken after 2000. The light-coloured area at the bottom of the rear fuselage is either the result of repairs or preparations for retrofitting chaff dispensers. (Holger Müller collection)

A typical spotter photo of the only Sri Lankan F-7 two-seater CTF703 without ground equipment and covers. The rear brake flap has been unhooked for maintenance work and only loosely connected to the associated hydraulic cylinder. (Holger Müller collection)

Two F-7GSs, followed by an F-7BS, in a flypast during the SLAF 60th Anniversary Exhibition in 2011. Due to the very small Sri Lankan F-7 fleet, both versions are operated jointly by No. 5 Jet Squadron. (Holger Müller)

F-7BS in the maintenance hangar in Katunayake. Noteworthy features include the chaff dispenser at the rear and the radar warning receiver antenna on the 'bulge' of the vertical stabiliser, neither of which were present when the aircraft was delivered and were therefore retrofitted at a later date. (Lukáš Syrovy via Jakub Fojtik)

Due to a lack of alternatives, the F-7s were soon deployed very intensively in the air-to-ground role. During one of these missions, two F-7s attacked a church in Jaffna in November 1993, killing up to 10 civilians. Because of the intensive use, a major overhaul was soon overdue and the aircraft had to be grounded at the end of the 1990s. It was not until 2003 that the overhaul took place in Pakistan. Afterwards, the F-7s resumed ground-attack missions alongside IAI Kfir C.2s and C.7s from Israel, which had been procured in the meantime. For this purpose, the aircraft were retrofitted with chaff and flare dispensers under the tail. Following the availability of MiG-27s from the Ukraine, the F/FT-7BS then stepped into their current role as advanced trainers. One aircraft, the F-7BS CF704, was lost on 23 July 2000.

When an LTTE Zlin Z143 bombed a Sri Lankan armed forces target for the first time in 2007, it became apparent that the SLAF had no aircraft type capable of countering this threat. The F-7BS did not have the equipment and armament to detect and engage such small targets, nor did it have the necessary low-speed capabilities to successfully engage these aircraft. Quickly, four F-7GS were procured from China, which were given the serials CF780–CF783.

The aircraft were equipped with a radar and PL-5 AAMs. In combination with the double-delta wing for improved flight characteristics at lower speeds, a weapon system was now available that was up to the new tasks and so the first success was not long in coming. On 9 September 2008, an LTTE Z143 was shot down by an F-7GS during a bombing raid. This is the first – and so far only – air victory in the history of the SLAF.

From 2009, the SLAF introduced a new designation system for its aeroplanes and helicopters. A combination of letters beginning with S for SLAF indicates the role of the respective type. The F-7s are categorised as Fighter Interceptors (SFI) and bear the serials SFI5101–SFI5103 (F-7BS) and SFI5104–SFI5106 and SFI5108 (F-7GS). The only FT-7BS had been assigned the serial SFT1401 as a fighter trainer.

Following the end of the fighting with the LTTE, the number of operational aircraft declined significantly. By 2017, the majority of Kfirs and MiG-27s were gradually decommissioned and the number of operational F-7s also dropped. In 2017, an F-7BS and an F-7GS were overhauled in China. The FT-7BS and another F-7GS were overhauled by the Aircraft Overhaul Wing in Katunayake, which was set up with the support of CATIC, and handed over to the SLAF on 10 July 2017.

The F-7s of the SLAF were involved in all recent Sri Lanka Independence Day parades at the beginning of February with two to three aircraft each, so that at least part of the fleet is still in service.

The F-7BS in the picture had the serial CF705 on delivery and was given the designation SFI (SLAF Fighter Interceptor) 5101 with the new designation system effective from 2009. The tail unit in the background with the serial SFI5106 belongs to an F-7GS. (Holger Müller)

This photograph of an F-7BS in a shelter in Katunayake was taken in 2023. The designation system has obviously been changed again, as the aircraft now bears its old number 705 with the new prefix SFI. The fresh paintwork and overall very good condition indicate that it has undergone industrial maintenance in the meantime. On this occasion, the aircraft's construction number was applied to the landing gear doors and wing spars. (Erik Sleutelberg)

A pair of F-7GSs with three 490-litre drop-tanks. The dark grey paint on the aircraft with the serial SFI5108, which also covers the drop-tank under the fuselage, was applied later and conceals previous special markings in this area. (Holger Müller)

F-7GS with the available range of weapons, covering both air-to-air and air-to-ground missions. (Holger Müller)

13

SUDAN

After around 100 years of British-Egyptian foreign rule, the independence of the Republic of Sudan was proclaimed in 1956. Until a Revolutionary Command Council took power and the associated shift to a pro-socialist course in 1969, Sudan's air arsenal consisted mainly of a few British aircraft. Sudan then received arms supplies from both China and the USSR. While the former only supplied F-5s (MiG-17s), 18 MiG-21Ms and four MiG-21USs arrived from the USSR in early 1970 to equip No. 2 Fighter Interceptor Squadron of the *Silakh al Jawwiya as Sudaniye* (Sudanese Air Force).

Following an attempted coup d'état against the then-ruling Jafar an-Numairi in 1971, all Soviet advisors were expelled from the country and bilateral relations were broken off. As a result of the end of spare parts deliveries, the operational readiness of the MiG-21 fleet declined rapidly. Heavy losses further decimated the fleet, the last of which were finally decommissioned in 1995.

Since the early 1980s, Sudan has pursued an Islamist course, which was continued by Umar Hasan Ahmad al-Bashir, who ruled the country from 1989 to 2019. Between 1983 and 2005, there was ongoing civil war in the country. There were also conflicts with neighbouring states. In 2011, the predominantly Christian-populated South Sudan seceded.

Sudan's changing foreign relations are reflected in the procurement of F-5s from the USA, F-6s and A-5s from China and MiG-29s from Russia, among others. In 2015 Sudan ordered six FTC-2000s, which were delivered in 2017 and entered service in May of the following year. The aircraft were given the serials 1201–1206 and are reportedly operated by the No. 66 Fighter Squadron at the Merowe (Marawi) base around 400 kilometres north of the capital Khartoum. However, as Merowe has hardly any infrastructure and no shelters, the aircraft may only be based there temporarily, for example during joint exercises with Egypt, and – like most other fighter aircraft types – are based at Wadi Sayyidna Air Base north of Khartoum. The Safat Aviation Complex, built at Wadi Sayyidna with Chinese support among others, provides maintenance capacity for these aircraft. There is no evidence that the FTC-2000 had been deployed as part of Sudan's involvement in the intervention in Yemen, which has been ongoing since 2015.

Since 15 April 2023, fighting has been raging in the country between the government troops of Abdel Fattah Burhan and the insurgent Rapid Support Forces (RSF) of his deputy Mohammed Hamdan Daglo. Immediately after the outbreak of hostilities, the RSF captured the Merowe Air Base on the Nile. One aircraft was destroyed in the fighting and at least one other damaged. On 24 May 2023, a third crashed or was shot down. The crew managed to escape. On 4 July, the loss of a fourth is reported, with only one pilot on board, who ejected and was subsequently captured by the RSF.

Sudanese FTC-2000 at the ceremonial commissioning. The access ladder next to the aircraft differs significantly from the models used on the MiG-21 and the classic J/F-7, which no longer fit due to the side air intake. (Sudan Defence Force)

Sudan's Chief of Staff, General Kamal Abdul Maaruf, inspects one of the new FTC-2000s. Despite the moderate image quality, the new HUD with two parallel screens is clearly visible. (Sudan Defence Force)

An FTC-2000 rolls in front of an Egyptian MiG-29 during a joint exercise at the Sudanese Merowe base in 2020. It is worth noting that the outer wing pylon for the drop-tanks has a straight leading edge like those classic J/F-7s, while on the inside the stepped version of the double-delta models is used. (Egyptian Ministry of Defence)

14

TANZANIA

In 1964, Tanzania was created from Tanganyika and Zanzibar, which gained their independence from Great Britain in 1961 and 1963, respectively. Under the leadership of Julius Nyerere, whose TANU party played an important role in the independence process, a one-party state was created in which a country-specific socialism was to be established. Nevertheless, the country enjoyed Western support for a long time, including from the Federal Republic of Germany and Canada, until the end of the 1960s when ever-closer ties with China put an end to this.

After a brief war with Uganda in 1971, the *Kamandi Ya Jeshi La Anga* (Tanzanian Air Force Command) initially received 22 FT-5s and 12 F-6s (MiG-17 and MiG-19, respectively) from China. In 1974, 14 MiG-21MFs and two MiG-21UMs arrived from the USSR. The rapid growth of the fleet overstretched the inexperienced armed forces of the economically weak country, leading to corresponding attrition. Nine or 10 MiG-21s, which survived the war against Uganda in 1978–79, had been parked in Mwanza on Lake Victoria since 1993.

For years thereafter, the JWTZ had only FT-5s, as well as FT-6s and further F-6s delivered in the meantime, until new F-7s in the form of 12 F-7TN single-seaters and two FT-7TN twin-seaters were ordered in 2009 and delivered in 2011. The aircraft were serialled JW9242–JW9253 (F-7TN) and JW9125–JW9126 (FT-7TN) and based in Ngerengere, about 100km west of the capital Dar-es-Salam. The single-seaters are operated by the Fighter Squadron, the twin-seaters by the Jet Training Squadron.

An F-7TN, probably JW9248, fell victim to a bird strike on 27 February 2015. The pilot managed to eject.

There are only a few high-resolution photos of the Tanzanian F-7s. This image was taken during a visit by the then President of Tanzania, John Magufuli, to the air force. If the photo is correctly dated to 2016, the immaculate condition of the aircraft suggests that they have seen very limited service. (JWTZ)

F-7TN with pods for unguided rockets and three drop-tanks, seen in overflight. It is not known which other weapons systems were delivered with the F/FT-7. (JWTZ)

The two Tanzanian two-seaters in flight. Due to the poor image quality, the serial numbers JW9125 (front) and JW9126 (rear) can only be guessed at. On the underside of the wings, both aircraft bear the letters TAFC for Tanzania Air Force Command in the largest possible letters, possibly to avoid being fired upon by their own troops in the event of conflict. No nationality markings are applied there. (Open source)

The Tanzanian President receives a briefing in the cockpit of the F-7TN. JWTZ aircraft only carry their serial number on the right side of the nose. The abbreviation TAFC on the right side stands for Tanzania Air Force Command. (JWTZ)

Tanzanian pilots with a Chinese instructor in front of their aircraft. One of the two FT-7TN two-seaters can be seen in the background on the right. While the combat aircraft are painted plain grey, the trainers feature a three-colour camouflage pattern (light brown, dark brown, blue-grey). (Open source)

15

USA

After the defeat of Germany and Japan in the Second World War, the USSR remained the only serious competitor to the USA. During the Cold War, which lasted more than 40 years and saw numerous heated conflicts develop between the two superpowers and their allies, the US armed forces suffered painful losses time and again, despite their massive personnel and technical superiority. Tactical deficits were identified as the cause of this – especially during the Vietnam War – and attempts were being made to eliminate them through realistic training. This included air combat training against so-called 'aggressors', pilots who used Soviet operational tactics and flying on indigenous aircraft types that were similar in their characteristics to Soviet aircraft. It was hoped that the high losses of pilots, particularly in the early phase of their deployment, would be reduced by confronting them with the enemy types of aircraft during training. This should counteract the so-called 'buck fever', the excitement of the first encounter, which often paralysed the pilot.

The prerequisite for such a programme was, of course, the availability of corresponding Soviet aircraft types. After the defected Iraqi MiG-21F-13 provided by Israel was extensively tested between January and April 1968 as part of Operation HAVE DOUGHNUT, it was thanks to General Suharto's taking of power in Indonesia in 1965 that a certain number of MiG-21s ended up in the hands of the US military.

The 6513th Test Squadron 'Red Hats' and the 4477th Test and Evaluation Flight (TEF, later T&E Squadron, TES) were set up for the technical and tactical evaluation of enemy aircraft types. From 1979 onwards, the latter unit, under code name CONSTANT PEG, carried out a realistic enemy simulation for US Air Force, Navy and Marine Corps pilots at the remote Tonopah base in the Nevada desert. This included demonstrations of the flying capabilities of enemy aircraft as well as simulated dogfights both individually and in groups. The flight characteristics of the MiG-21 were rated by the participating pilots as exceptionally good and superior to most of the contemporary US types.

Officially, only the deployment of the Indonesian MiG-21F-13 – 10 aircraft in total – has been confirmed so far. In 1978 the Egyptians, who under President Sadat had turned away from the USSR and towards the Americans, handed over 16 MiG-21MFs to the USAF. Finally, in 1987, in a phase of rapprochement between the two countries, 12 (according to other sources 15) F-7Bs were procured directly from China. The remaining Soviet-built MiG-21F-13s were then decommissioned. Precise information on the procurement of the F-7B remains classified to this day. However, various photographs of the F-7B in US colours confirm the fact of its use. During their service with the 4477th TES, the MiG-21s were given the designations YF-110B (F-13), YF-110C (F-7B) and YF-110D (MF) in order to not to give any indication of the actual type of aircraft. The national insignia in the form of red stars and the two-digit serials (bort numbers) common in Soviet air regiments (whereby one aircraft also bore a three-digit number, the numbers 57, 68, 69, 75, 96, 99 and 300 are known for the F-7B) also did not allow any conclusions to be drawn about the actual user. It is not known whether the aircraft received the regular USAF serial, consisting of the fiscal year of procurement and consecutive number.

The maintenance of the aircraft was carried out by hand-picked technicians and – in the case of the engines – by General Electric.

While the original plan was to procure enough aircraft to simulate two Soviet air defence regiments, the programme was terminated in March 1988 in view of the onset of détente and the increasingly costly maintenance of the aircraft. By then, more than 15,000 flights had been completed and around 6,000 crews had been trained. Prior to this, the 4477th TES had retired from active service with a simultaneous deployment of 13 MiG-21/F-7Bs and four MiG-23s on a Red Flag manoeuvre. Despite a tight spare parts situation – only a few critical components, such as pyro-cartridges for the ejection seats, were replicated by US companies – and a lack of technical documents, only one MiG-21F-13, but no F-7B, was lost in service. It is not until November 2006 that the secrecy surrounding CONSTANT PEG was lifted and the use of MiG-21s and F-7s in this operation was officially confirmed.

Some of the MiG-21F-13s ended up in museums. However, F-7Bs that can be linked to CONSTANT PEG have not yet appeared in museums. Supposedly, the F-7Bs were buried in the desert near their former base.

Probably not least because of their very short service life – there was only one year between their procurement in 1987 and the end of the CONSTANT PEG programme – there are far fewer pictures of the F-7B available than of the MiG-21F-13. This screenshot is taken from a video that recently appeared on YouTube showing several of these aircraft in action. (US DoD)

Like all other foreign types in the inventory of the 4477th Test and Evaluation Flight, the F-7Bs carried Soviet-style nationality markings and serials. Some aircraft, such as the 96 shown here, were painted in camouflage, while others flew in their standard white livery. The pilot's name can be seen under the cockpit (but could not be deciphered due to the image resolution) and the unit's internal aircraft number 47 could be seen on the nose landing gear door. (US DoD)

16

ZIMBABWE

Alongside Zambia and Malawi, Zimbabwe emerged from the federation of Rhodesia and Nyasaland, which was dissolved at the end of 1963. With the declaration of independence in 1965, a civil war began between the white government and the African guerrilla organisations ZANU (under the leadership of the later president Robert Mugabe) and ZAPU (under Joshua Nkomo). This war was only ended in 1980 by a ceasefire and the internationally recognised independence of the country.

Until 1980, the Rhodesian Air Force was largely equipped with British equipment. After independence, the air force, now called the Air Force of Zimbabwe (AFZ), was reorganised with Pakistani support. In 1986–87, Chengdu Aircraft Factory delivered four F-7Bs (serials 700–703) and eight F-7IINs (704–711) to the AFZ. At least the F-7Bs were provided by China free of charge. Initially, China took over the training of pilots and technicians. The AFZ, which had to accept considerable losses of experienced personnel, was supported in F-7 operations by Pakistani exchange pilots.

The F-7s were delivered by sea and assembled by Chinese technicians at Thornhill Air Base near the central Zimbabwean town of Gweru. The aircraft equipped the newly-created No. 5 Squadron at this base. In 1991, two two-seater FT-7BZs (730 and 731) joined the unit. Initially FT-5s were used for training purposes, later BAe Hawks fulfilled this task and today the pilots train on Chinese K-8s before switching to the F-7.

According to unconfirmed reports, the F-7s flew their first missions in support of the Mozambican government against the RENAMO rebels immediately after their delivery, operating from bases in the neighbouring country.

There is contradictory information on the alleged deployment of the F-7 during the AFZ's involvement on the side of President Kabila in the civil war in the Democratic Republic of Congo (formerly Zaire). It is highly probable that only the BAe Hawks of the AFZ, which were better suited to the air-to-ground role, were used here. In any case, the reports of losses suffered by the F-7 fleet are questionable. Between August 1998 and March 1999, the anti-Kabila rebels reported the shooting-down of a total of six Zimbabwean F-7s. It was only after the end of hostilities that the AFZ definitely lost F-7s in the Congo, when three aircraft crashed on the way to the funeral for the assassinated President Kabila in 2001. One crashed in a tropical storm, but the pilot managed to eject. Another made a belly landing and the third overshot the runway. The latter two aircraft were recovered and repaired. Prior to this, two F-7s – F-7B 700 on 14 November 1994 and another on 27 February 1995 – had already been lost in accidents.

Reports that Zimbabwe, despite its extremely poor economic situation, had subsequently received a further 12 F-7MGs from China were just as false as those about the procurement of MiG-29s and JF-17s. Rather, the existing F-7s underwent a limited modernisation, externally recognisable by new antennas.

After the F/FT-7 fleet had been grounded for some time, at least some of the aircraft were made airworthy again for the air parade on the occasion of Zimbabwe Defence Forces (ZDF) Day in August 2019. One aircraft (708) that was no longer airworthy now serves as a training aid in Harare.

The remaining F/FT-7s are still operated by No. 5 Squadron at Gweru-Thornhill, which was renamed Josiah Tungamirai Air Force Base in 2018. On 30 May 2025, F-7B 703 crashed there. The pilot who was killed in the crash is said to be a reactivated veteran of the Congo War, which indicates a shortage of operational pilots.

Zimbabwean F-7IIN in the delivery paint scheme. Initially the aircraft carried a fin flash in the shape of a bird on the vertical stabiliser, which was later replaced by the national flag. (Ian Malcolm)

In the front cockpit of FT-7BZ 730, the hood, which is extended during instrument flight training and restricts the student pilot's view of the surroundings, is clearly visible . The aircraft carries a 720-litre drop-tank under the fuselage. While this tank has the same colour as the aircraft, all 490-litre tanks of the AFZ are unpainted. (Ian Malcolm)

Two F-7IINs fly over Charles Prince Airport north of Harare during an air show held by a local flying club on 7 May 1995. Such public appearances are rather rare. (Winston Brent)

A formation of one FT-7BZ and two F-7IINs in flight. While the fin flash on the two aircraft in the foreground has already been replaced by the flag, the leading aircraft still carries it. (Open source)

F-7B 702 wears the grey and white paint scheme that was applied to all aircraft during a later overhaul. The instrument landing system (ILS) antenna on the side was added to the aircraft as part of an upgrade. (Open source)

The personal aircraft of the long-standing commander of No. 5 Squadron, Flt. Lt. Michael Enslin, not only carries his name and rank under the cockpit, but also a personal coat of arms, which can be found on the helmet too. (Open source)

The FT-7BZ 730 and several other F-7s were restored to flying condition after a long period of inactivity for the 40th anniversary of the AFZ and took part in a "mass flypast" over Harare in 2019. (AFZ)

APPENDICES

China Aviation Industry Corporation (AVIC)

In order to organise the development of the Chinese aviation industry, a corresponding structure was created at an early stage, which was repeatedly subject to structural changes over the course of time. In accordance with the leading role of the Communist Party and the country's centralised administration, all fundamental decisions were taken at the highest level of the party and state leadership. It is less important for an understanding of the actual process which body made a particular decision, which is why such details are not mentioned here.

By resolution of the Military Commission of the Central Committee of the Communist Party of China on 17 April 1951, the Aviation Industry Bureau was established within the Ministry of Heavy Machinery as the first management body for the planned industry. At the same time, an Aviation Industry Organisation Commission was established, which reported directly to the Military Commission. After the Aviation Industry Office was repeatedly assigned to other ministries, a unified management body for the aviation industry was created in September 1963 in the form of a separate ministry. In future, all planning processes for the aviation industry were to be concentrated in this Third Ministry of Machine-Building and the work of the companies was to be directed and monitored by the new authority.

From 1982 onwards the organisation was referred to as the Ministry of Aviation Industry or the Aerospace Industry (from 1988). In the course of China's economic reforms, the ministry was transformed into a group of companies under the name China Aviation Industry Corporation. The division into two structures called China Aviation Industry Corporation I and II (AVIC I and II) in 1999 was reversed in 2008. Since then, the umbrella organisation of the Chinese aviation industry has operated under the name Aviation Industry Corporation of China.

Shenyang Aircraft Factory

The State Aircraft Factory 112 in Shenyang (formerly known as Mukden) is the oldest production site in the Chinese aviation industry. Built with Soviet assistance in accordance with the treaty signed between China and the USSR in May 1953, the plant first produced the MiG-17 as the J-5 and then the MiG-19 as the J-6. The complex also included an engine factory at the same site.

As the most experienced and technologically leading production facility in China, the plant was given the task of taking over the licence production of the MiG-21 and started preparing for production on the basis of Soviet design drawings and technological information. The pattern aircraft and MiG-21 CKD kits from the USSR were also delivered to Shenyang. Even after the decision of the political leadership to concentrate on the large-scale production of the J-6, Plant No. 112 continued to take over the technological preparation of production, the assembly of the 15 CKD kits, the production of a first batch of four prototypes and finally, at the end of 1967, small scale production of the J-7, which ended in 1970 after 23 aircraft.

Afterwards, the Shenyang aircraft plant gradually handed over production to the two new production sites in Chengdu and Guizhou and supported them with sample parts, design drawings, process information and material samples. Shenyang then focussed on the manufacture of the J-8 heavy fighter aircraft.

Today, around 15,000 employees in Shenyang manufacture Chinese versions of the Su-27 as the J-11, J-15 and J-16, the J-35 stealth fighter, components for Boeing, BAE Systems, Airbus and Bombardier, as well as buses and other non-aerospace products.

Chengdu Aircraft Factory

The construction of State Aircraft Factory No. 132 in Chengdu in Sichuan Province was part of the agreement signed in April 1956 between the governments of China and the USSR on a second series of 19 construction projects to support the Chinese aviation industry. Construction of the factory officially began on 18 October 1958 and was essentially completed by 1964.

Although development of the plant was still underway at this time, production of the MiG-17PF as the J-5A began there in 1961, followed later by the twin-seater JJ-5 derived from it. The maiden flight of a J-5 built in Chengdu took place in November 1964. In June 1965, the Chengdu Aircraft Factory was ordered to prepare the production of the J-7 in addition to the J-5A and JJ-5. This necessitated a major technical reorganisation of the factory, which was not completed until the end of 1968, when series production of the J-7 was ready to start. At this time, when the Cultural Revolution was raging in China, the factory was under the administration of the People's Liberation Army. This situation lasted until 1972. During this period, production of the slightly modified J-7I began, followed in 1979 by the successor variant, the J-7II. In order to ensure the smooth running of series production of the J-7, the Chengdu Aircraft Factory again carried out a comprehensive technical reorganisation at the end of the 1970s, combined with a massive expansion of the factory. The work was not completed until 1985. According to Chinese figures, the production capacity was then around 200 J-7s per year.

At this time, the Chengdu Aircraft Factory also produced a wide range of civilian products such as vehicles, household appliances, windows and tools. These activities were outsourced to separate companies in the 1990s. Parallel to the production of the modernised F-7M in the second half of the 1980s, the plant began supplying components for civil aircraft, initially to McDonnell-Douglas in the USA. Since 1989, the company has operated under the name Chengdu Aircraft Industrial Corporation.

Parallel to the production of the J-7E between 1993 and 2001 and the J-7G based on it between 2002 and 2013, the successor models J-10 for domestic use and JF-17 for export were developed. Both the J-10, which made its maiden flight in 1998, and the JF-17, which flew for the first time in 2003, were designed with foreign support from Israel and Russia, respectively. Production runs since 2002 and 2006 respectively – for the JF-17 in a work share with Pakistan Aeronautical Complex (PAC) Kamra.

Today, the J-20 stealth model is manufactured. In addition, the plant in Chengdu produces components for Airbus, Boeing and Dassault as well as for the Chinese ARJ21 passenger aircraft, and also automotive components.

Production of the J-7II in Chengdu in the 1980s. (Chinese Internet)

The same halls in the 1990s when the J-7E was built. The equipment in the workshops has not changed significantly. (Chinese Internet)

The Chengdu Aircraft Industrial (Group) Company Limited, which had existed since 1998, includes the actual aircraft factory, the Chengdu Engine Company (Chengdu Aero-Engine), the Chengdu Aircraft Design Institute founded in 1970 and the Wenjiang airfield.

Guizhou Aircraft Plant

The construction of the Guizhou Aircraft Manufacturing Base (Base 011, Plant 162) was part of the third stage of the state plan to develop the aviation industry and began in November 1964 in Guiyang and Anshun in Guizhou province. The complex, which was completed in 1970, was intended as a reserve production facility for the relocation of J-7 production from the Shenyang aircraft plant. At the same time, the Guizhou Liyang engine plant (Plant 460), which is part of the factory, was to take over production of the WP-7 engine from the Shenyang engine plant. While the latter succeeded, the start of J-7 production was halted and the Guizhou Aircraft Factory concentrated on the production of the J-6III.

The era of the J-7 only began in Guizhou with the J-7II, which was produced there between 1982 and 1986. For the J-7III, which was only produced in small numbers, Guizhou acted as a supplier of components, including the wings. After production and further development of the WP-7 in the meantime, Guizhou Engine Design Institute and Liyang Engine Plant prepared the reverse engineering of the R13-300 engine as WP-13 and subsequently produced it for use in all newer J-7 versions.

Parallel to the production of the single-seaters, Guizhou took over the design work for the JJ-7 two-seater from 1981, although small series production of this aircraft did not start until 1988. The development and production of the subsequent FT-7P (from 1989) and the JJ-7A (from 1994) then also took place exclusively in Guizhou. The end of series production of the latter on 26 September 2016 also marked the end of production of the MiG-21 in its original shape worldwide.

Since 2007, low rate initial production of the successor model JL-9/FTC-2000 developed there had been running in Guizhou, which was transferred to series production when assembly of the FT-7 for export ended in 2013. Today, the improved JL-9G and FTC-2000G are manufactured, as well as AAMs and drones. The plant is also involved in the production of the JF-17, including the WS-13 engine, which replaces the original Russian RD-93.

GAIC has more than 40 subcontractors and suppliers with a total of over 50,000 employees, including four aircraft factories, seven engine manufacturers and 10 production facilities each for aircraft equipment and mechanical components. The larger and better-known ones include the aforementioned final producers Yunma Aircraft Manufacturing Factory and Guizhou Liyang Aero-Engine Corporation.

In addition to aviation-related products, GAIC's sub-companies also supply numerous other items, such as lorries, buses and trams.

China National Aero-Technology Import and Export Corporation (CATIC)

Before 1978, China provided ideologically motivated military aid, usually free of charge. Since 1958, the Chinese aviation industry has supplied more than 1,000 aircraft and associated spare parts to 16 countries. In the course of the economic reforms, the Chinese leadership decided to change from the original free military aid to a staggered system of sales, bartering and gifts. The China National Aero-Technology Import and Export Corporation (CATIC), founded on 18 January 1979, took over the commercial handling of the import and export of aviation products.

In 2008, the organisation was restructured and renamed AVIC INTERNATIONAL. However, the name CATIC is retained, as the organisation now operates exclusively for military exports under this name.

The Men Behind the Scenes

As with the Soviet original, comparatively little is known about the designers of the J/F-7. For example, the names Mikoyan and Gurevich are usually linked to the MiG-21, as they were the founders of the design bureau in which the aircraft was developed, while the name of the MiG-21 chief designer, Anatoly Grigoryevich Brunov, is only rarely mentioned. And only key points are known about his life.

In connection with the Chinese MiG-21 derivative, the names of individuals do not appear at all in the type designations, as the individual versions are designated exclusively by a combination of letters and numbers. In foreign publications, these are usually preceded by the manufacturer's plant, i.e. Shenyang, Chengdu or Guizhou. Nevertheless, there are of course people who had a decisive influence on the development of the aircraft family, though no more is known about these men (without exception) in key positions than their names. Peng Renying, for example, was named as chief designer of the F-7B and subsequently associated with both the J-7IIA and the F-7M/F-7MP. Chief designers of the J-7III were Wang Shounan and later Song Wencong. Yu Xuiming acted as chief designer of the JJ-7, Wu Binglin as that of the FT-7P. Lu Yuying was named as chief designer of the J-7IIH, F-7MP and J-7E, while Song Kaiji was only associated with the former type. The J-7G was developed under the direction of chief designer Song Chengzhi. Finally, Hu Jinxing was the lead designer of the FTC-2000G.

A little more is known about Tu Jida than about most of his colleagues. Tu, who had already led the development of the J-5A and JJ-5 as chief designer, was the victim of persecution and maltreatment during the Cultural Revolution. He was only allowed to return to work at the end of 1969 and took over the development of the J-7I. It was said to be thanks to his pragmatic approach that the initially unrealisable requirements were reduced and a version suitable for series production was created with the J-7I 'three modifications'. Later, he was also responsible for the J-7II, J-7IIA and J/F-7M. He also taught at the Aerospace University of Nanjing.

Song Wencong, one of the aforementioned chief designers of the less successful J-7III, became better known through the development of China's first truly modern fighter aircraft, the J-10, which he led from 1986.

Tu Jida was probably the most distinguished of the J/F-7 designers, as the aircraft family owed the successful start of series production to his pragmatic approach in the early stages of development. (Chinese Internet)

Song Wengcong led the development of the J-7III together with Wang Shounan, but only became known to a wider audience as the chief designer of the J-10. (Chinese Internet)

Construction Numbers/Batch Sizes

Among the questions that cannot be definitively answered due to a lack of information are the exact number of aircraft produced, the construction number system and the associated batch sizes. While the construction number system of Soviet MiG-21s could be largely deciphered on the basis of the fleet lists of European users alone, before corresponding information was available from Soviet/Russian sources, both information from the manufacturers and sufficiently comprehensive and detailed data on the users' inventories are still missing for Chinese aircraft.

Nevertheless, at least some basic statements can be made about the numbering systems of the individual works.

Shenyang Aircraft Factory

For the initially assembled CKD, Shenyang factory obviously used their Soviet construction numbers. This is at least suggested by the information given for surviving aircraft, such as the MiG-21F-13 with serial 98071 displayed in Datangshan. Various sources agree that the aircraft was given the construction number 1623, which according to the allocation scheme of aircraft factory No. 21 in Gorky was then 74211623.

However, the construction numbers 714611 and 714619, which are regularly given for J-7 11244 and 11447 displayed in Datangshan, are somewhat dubious. With the exception of the retrofitted brake chute container, both aircraft are externally similar to the MiG-21F-13, i.e. they were built in Shenyang.

Finally, the J-7s that Albania received as military aid in 1970 were also manufactured in Shenyang. The construction numbers of these aircraft are not known, but their serials are. As the gap in the allocation of these numbers (from 0210 to 0304) can hardly be explained otherwise, it can be assumed that the serials are also the construction numbers. These four-digit numbers, each with two digits for batch and serial number within the batch, correspond to those used in Shenyang for the preceding J-6 as well as the subsequent J-8, such as J6-4702 or J8-0208. In contrast to other types, the number of aircraft was probably limited to 10 per batch, as otherwise the batch number 03 would not have been achievable with a total production of only 39 aircraft. In addition, the aircraft assembled from CKD must have been included in this count (i.e. they may have had both a Soviet and a Chinese construction number).

Table 2: Known Construction numbers for aircraft produced at the Shenyang Aircraft Factory

Construction number	Serial	Version	Country
74211623	98071	MiG-21F-13	China
714611	11244	J-7	China
714619	11447	J-7	China
J7-0201	0201	J-7	Albania
J7-0202	0202	J-7	Albania
J7-0203	0203	J-7	Albania
J7-0204	0204	J-7	Albania
J7-0205	0205	J-7	Albania
J7-0206	0206	J-7	Albania
J7-0207	0207	J-7	Albania
J7-0209	0209	J-7	Albania
J7-0210	0210	J-7	Albania
J7-0304	0304	J-7	Albania

Chengdu Aircraft Factory

Although the available construction numbers of J/F-7s from the Chengdu Aircraft Factory are significantly more numerous than those from Shenyang, they only allow for more-or-less qualified assumptions in view of the significantly higher output.

In the production of the J-7I, initially in the 'six modifications', then in the 'three modifications' variant, a five-digit and later a six-digit construction number was used, with the change taking place from the ninth to the tenth production batch.

For the subsequent J-7II, counting of the batches started again at zero and the actual four-digit construction number, consisting of two digits for each the batch and the consecutive number in the batch, was incremented continuously – regardless of whether it was a domestic J-7II or an export F-7B. The version was differentiated by a number-letter prefix (72, 72H, 7BS, 72K).

Construction number 72M1203 of J-7IIM (12284) on display at Datangshan Museum indicates that the actual construction number was retained in subsequent modifications, but the version prefix was changed.

With the subsequent generations of F-7M, J-7III and J-7E, the counting was restarted, whereby the numbering of the J-7III (J-7C) was also continued for the J-7IIIA (J-7D – here with the change of the batch number from 0 to 1) and that of the J-7E for both the J-7G and the export versions based on it. With the exception of the J-7III/IIIA, the batch size was probably 40 aircraft. At least 40 is the highest known sequential number. If all batches up to the highest known number have been produced with 40 aircraft each, this results in possible quantities of 1,160 J-7II/F-7B (batches 0 to 28, whereby the 'official' production figures are much lower, which suggests gaps in the numbering), 320 J-7E (batches 0 to 7) and 85 J-7G (25 plus three aircraft of batch 9, 21 plus 13 aircraft of batch 10, 11 plus 12 aircraft of batch 11), whereby batches 7 to 9 probably also included the Pakistani F-7PG, of which no constructions numbers are known. However, it is unclear whether the batches were produced in their entirety. For the last batch 11, the limit of 40 aircraft was overruled and counting continues beyond that, so that the highest construction number of this batch and that of the last single-seat J/F-7 built is 1163.

Table 3: Known Construction numbers for aircraft produced at the Chengdu Aircraft Factory

Construction number	Serial	Version	Country
70004	3487	J-7I 6A	China
70009	80139	J-7I	China
70703	12381	J-7I	China
70705	12284	J-7I	China
701008		J-7I	DPRK
701017		J-7I	DPRK
720040		J-7II	China
720412	4656	J-7II	China
720612		J-7II	China
720716		J-7II	China
720735		J-7II	China
720812		J-7II	China
720819		J-7II	China
721102		J-7II	China
721131		J-7II	China
72M1203	12284	J-7IIM	China
721221		J-7II	China
721236	73x7x	J-7II	China
72H1323		J-7IIH	China
721337		J-7II	China
721426		J-7II	China
72H1533		J-7IIH	China
72H1737		J-7IIH	China
72H2207	70327	J-7IIH	China
72H2230		J-7IIH	China
7BS2237	CF704	F-7BS	Sri Lanka
7BS2238	CF705	F-7BS	Sri Lanka
7BS2239	CF707	F-7BS	Sri Lanka
7BS2240	CF708	F-7BS	Sri Lanka
72H2303		J-7IIH	China
72H2325		J-7IIH	China
72H2325		J-7IIH	China
72H2402		J-7IIH	China
72K2828	1654	F-7IIK	Myanmar
7MB0413	1413	F-7MB	Bangladesh
7MB0414	1414	F-7MB	Bangladesh
7MB0415	1415	F-7MB	Bangladesh
7MB0416	1416	F-7MB	Bangladesh
7MB0417	1417	F-7MB	Bangladesh
7MB0418	1418	F-7MB	Bangladesh
7MB0419	1419	F-7MB	Bangladesh
7MB0420	1420	F-7MB	Bangladesh
7MB0421	1421	F-7MB	Bangladesh
7MB0422	1422	F-7MB	Bangladesh
7MB0423	1423	F-7MB	Bangladesh
7MB0424	1424	F-7MB	Bangladesh
7MB0425	1425	F-7MB	Bangladesh
7MB0426	1426	F-7MB	Bangladesh
7MB0427	1427	F-7MB	Bangladesh
7MB0428	1428	F-7MB	Bangladesh
730002		J-7III	China
730005		J-7C	China
730010	69492	J-7III	China
730011	69493	J-7III	China
730013	69495	J-7III	China
730015	69497	J-7III	China
73A0102	21002	J-7IIIA	China
73A0117?	21109	J-7IIIA	China
7D0124	30169	J-7D	China
7E0001	40713	J-7E	China
7E0001	72263	J-7E	China
7E0114		J-7E	China
7EH0205		J-7EH	China
7E0212		J-7E	China
7E0221		J-7E	China
7E0227	30169	J-7E	China
7E0320	32293	J-7E	China
7E0321		J-7E	China
7E0322	12228	J-7E	China
7E0408		J-7E	China
7E0427			China
7EH0440		J-7EH	China
7E0502		J-7E	China
7E0612	21251	J-7E	China
7E0618?	70086	J-7E	China
7EB0631		J-7EB	China
7EB0632		J-7EB	China
7EB0633		J-7EB	China

Construction number	Serial	Version	Country
7EB0636	41287	J-7EB	China
7EB0701		J-7EB	China
0926	0310*	F-7NM	Namibia
0927	0313*	F-7NM	Namibia
0928	0315*	F-7NM	Namibia
0929	0317*	F-7NM	Namibia
0930	0319*	F-7NM	Namibia
0931	0321*	F-7NM	Namibia
0932	932	F-7BG	Bangladesh
0933	933	F-7BG	Bangladesh
0934	934	F-7BG	Bangladesh
0935	935	F-7BG	Bangladesh
0936	936	F-7BG	Bangladesh
0937	937	F-7BG	Bangladesh
7GB1006		J-7GB	China
7GB1008	11	J-7GB	China
7G1017		J-7G	China
7G1018		J-7G	China
1022	938	F-7BG	Bangladesh
1023	939	F-7BG	Bangladesh
1024	940	F-7BG	Bangladesh
1025	941	F-7BG	Bangladesh
1026	942	F-7BG	Bangladesh
1027	943	F-7BG	Bangladesh
7G1035	65x5x	J-7G	China
7G1038		J-7G	China
1112	SFI5104	F-7GS	Sri Lanka
1113	SFI5105	F-7GS	Sri Lanka
1114	SFI5106	F-7GS	Sri Lanka
1115	SFI5108	F-7GS	Sri Lanka
7G1121		J-7G	China
1128	NAF800	F-7NI	Nigeria
1129	NAF801	F-7NI	Nigeria
1130	NAF802	F-7NI	Nigeria
1131	NAF803	F-7NI	Nigeria
1132	NAF804	F-7NI	Nigeria
1133	NAF805	F-7NI	Nigeria
1134	NAF806	F-7NI	Nigeria
1135	NAF807	F-7NI	Nigeria
1136	NAF808	F-7NI	Nigeria
1137	NAF809	F-7NI	Nigeria
1138	NAF810	F-7NI	Nigeria
1139	NAF811	F-7NI	Nigeria
1140	9242	F-7TG	Tanzania
1141	9243	F-7TG	Tanzania
1142	9244	F-7TG	Tanzania
1143	9245	F-7TG	Tanzania
1144	9246	F-7TG	Tanzania
1145	9247	F-7TG	Tanzania
1146	9248	F-7TG	Tanzania
1147	9249	F-7TG	Tanzania
1148	9250	F-7TG	Tanzania
1149	9251	F-7TG	Tanzania
1150	9252	F-7TG	Tanzania
1151	9253	F-7TG	Tanzania
1152	2711	F-7BGI	Bangladesh
1153	2712	F-7BGI	Bangladesh
1154	2713	F-7BGI	Bangladesh
1155	2714	F-7BGI	Bangladesh
1156	2715	F-7BGI	Bangladesh
1157	2716	F-7BGI	Bangladesh
1158	2717	F-7BGI	Bangladesh
1159	2718	F-7BGI	Bangladesh
1160	2719	F-7BGI	Bangladesh
1161	2720	F-7BGI	Bangladesh
1162	2721	F-7BGI	Bangladesh
1163	2722	F-7BGI	Bangladesh

* For the Namibian F-7NMs, the serials were probably not assigned in the order of the construction numbers. Construction number 0927 is given for 0315 that was involved in the accident, 0926 for 0310 and 0925 for 0319. However, the author has no reliable proof of this. The range of construction numbers given for the Namibian aircraft from 0926 to 0931 is probably correct.

Guizhou Aircraft Factory

The factory in Guizhou used separate number ranges for the single-seaters (J-7II exclusively for domestic use) and double-seaters (all versions for domestic and export) produced there. The J-7IIs produced in Guizhou were likely to include all those whose five-digit construction number scheme did not fit into the one used in Chengdu. In view of only two available numbers (60616, 70703), further analyses are unnecessary.

A scheme similar to that of the Chengdu plant was used for the two-seaters. The counting of the batches starts at zero and the four-digit construction number, consisting of two digits for each batch and consecutive number in the batch, is counted up continuously. Domestic and export versions follow each other alternately. One or two preceding letters (A, S, T, and TP) are used to differentiate between versions. The batches here probably comprised a maximum of 20 aircraft, as 20 is the highest known consecutive number. Twenty-two known batches (0 to 21) result in a possible output of 440 aircraft. The prefix 'A' seems to have no reference to the JJ-7A version but is generally used for all JJ-7s. For the JL-9/FTC-2000, the count starts from the beginning, with both variants alternating. However, the batch size is obviously different, as 45 appears as the largest consecutive number.

Table 4: Known Construction Numbers for aircraft produced at the Guizhou Aircraft Factory

Construction number	Serial	Version	Country
60616		J-7II	China
70703	12381	J-7II	China
A0001		JJ-7	China
A0002		JJ-7	Pakistan
S0005		FT-7BS	Sri Lanka
A0105		FT-7A	Pakistan
L0206	4453	JJ-7A	China
A0207	21304	JJ-7A	China
A0208?	21325	JJ-7A	China
T0402?	730	FT-7B	Zimbabwe
A0511	3610	JJ-7A	China
A0517	3615	JJ-7A	China

Construction number	Serial	Version	Country
A0601	74537	JJ-7A	China
T0605	2432	FT-7B	Bangladesh
A0605?		JJ-7A	China
A0607		JJ-7A	China
L0607	2528	JJ-7A	China
A0718	3316	JJ-7A	China
L0801	40235	JJ-7A	China
L0811		JJ-7A	China
A0817	74x3x	JJ-7A	China
A0819	xx6x3	JJ-7A	China
L0820		JJ-7?	China
TP0919		FT-7P	China
A0919		JJ-7A	China
A0920		JJ-7A	China
L1013	74636	JJ-7A	China
L1015	4351	JJ-7A	China
L1016	40233	JJ-7A	China
L1017	2622	JJ-7A	China
A1018		JJ-7A	China
L1019	40239	JJ-7A	China
A1020	70127	JJ-7A	China
L1120		JJ-7A	China
TP1203	3-7718	FT-7N	Iran
TP1204	3-7719	FT-7N	Iran
A1207	21306	JJ-7A	China
A1214	4355	JJ-7A	China
L1305	40231	JJ-7A	China
L1414	3517	JJ-7A	China
T1415	2434	FT-7B	Bangladesh
T1416	2435	FT-7B	Bangladesh
L1417		JJ-7?	China
L1508		JJ-7?	China
L1509	3516	JJ-7A	China
L1515	3518	JJ-7A	China
T1601	2436	FT-7B	Bangladesh

Construction number	Serial	Version	Country
L1607	3514	JJ-7A	China
L1609	3516	JJ-7A	China
TP1707	NAF812	FT-7NI	Nigeria
TP1708	NAF813	FT-7NI	Nigeria
TP1904	?	FT-7NM	Namibia
TP1906	F944	FT-7BG	Bangladesh
TP1907	F945	FT-7BG	Bangladesh
TP1908	F946	FT-7BG	Bangladesh
TP1909	F947	FT-7BG	Bangladesh
TP1910	NAF014	FT-7NI	Nigeria
P2101	2701	FT-7BGI	Bangladesh
P2102	2702	FT-7BGI	Bangladesh
P2103	2703	FT-7BGI	Bangladesh
P2104	2704	FT-7BGI	Bangladesh
JL90001	421	JL-9	China
JL90002		JL-9	China
JL90003	422	JL-9	China
JL90104		JL-9	China
JL90207		JL-9	China
JL90509	4086	JL-9	China
JL90621		JL-9	China
JL90640	1x3x	JL-9	China
JL90706	1139	JL-9	China
J0741	1201	FTC-2000	Sudan
J0745	1205	FTC-2000	Sudan
JL90804		JL-9	China
JL90815		JL-9	China
JL90818	1213	JL-9	China
FT-9G10101	1401	FTC-2000G	Myanmar
FT-9G10102	1402	FTC-2000G	Myanmar
FT-9G10103	1403	FTC-2000G	Myanmar
FT-9G10104	1404	FTC-2000G	Myanmar
FT-9G10105	1405	FTC-2000G	Myanmar
FT-9G10106	1406	FTC-2000G	Myanmar

SELECTED BIBLIOGRAPHY

A 187 / 1 / 123 Flugzeug 66 – Zelle: Nationale Volksarmee der DDR 1968

A 187 / 1 / 128 Flugzeug MiG-21PF – Betriebsvorschrift – Teil I – Zelle – Triebwerk – Bildband: Nationale Volksarmee der DDR, Kommando der LSK /LV 1967

Anon, *China Today: Aviation Industry* (Beijing: China Aviation Industry Press, 1989)

Brent, Winston, *African Air Forces* (Nelspruit: Freeworld Publications, 1999)

Cooper, Tom and Bishop, Farzad, *Iran-Iraq War in the Air* (Atglen: Schiffer, 2000)

Cooper, Tom and Weinert, Peter, with Fabian Hinz and Mark Lepko, *African MiGs Volume 1 – Angola to Ivory Coast* (Houston: Harpia Publishing, 2010)

Cooper, Tom and Weinert, Peter, with Fabian Hinz and Mark Lepko, *African MiGs Volume 2 – Madagascar to Zimbabwe* (Houston: Harpia Publishing, 2011)

Cooper, Tom, Babak Taghvaee, and Liam Devlin, *IRIAF 2010* (Houston: Harpia Publishing, 2010)

Davies, Steve, *Red Eagles: America's Secret MiGs* (Oxford: Osprey Publishing, 2008)

Fontanellaz, Adrien, *Paradise Afire Volume 3: The Sri Lankan War 1990 – 1994* (Warwick: Helion & Company 2020)

Hewson, Robert, *Jane's Weapons: Air-Launched 2014 – 2015* (Coulsdon: IHS, 2014)

Kim, Kuk-ch'ŏl (ed), *Immortal history of DPRK-PRC friendship* (Pyongyang: Foreign Languages Publishing House of the DPR Korea, 2022)

Matoulek, Ovčačik, Pavlovský, Susa, *MiG-21F/U* (Prague: 4+, 2008) (in Czech)

Mitzer, Stijn, Oliemans, Joost, *The Armed Forces of North Korea* (Warwick: Helion & Company, 2020)

Müller, Holger, *MiG-21* (2nd edition) (Stuttgart: Motorbuch Verlag, 2022) (in German)

Müller, Holger, *MiG-21 im Einsatz – Teil 1: Süd- und Südostasien: FLiEGERREVUE extra 21* (Berlin: Möller Buch und Zeitschriften Verlag, 2008)

Müller, Holger, *MiG-21 im Einsatz – Teil 2: Naher Osten und Arabien: FLiEGERREVUE extra 23* (Berlin: Möller Buch und Zeitschriften Verlag, 2008)

Müller, Holger, *MiG-21 im Einsatz – Teil 3: Schwarzafrika und Amerika: FLiEGERREVUE extra 25* (Berlin: Möller Buch und Zeitschriften Verlag, 2009)

Müller, Holger, *Sri Lankas Luftwaffe wurde 60: FliegerRevue Extra 33* (Bergkirchen: PPV Medien, 2011)

Sadik, Ahmad, Cooper, Tom, *Iraqi Fighters 1953-2003: Camouflage & Markings* (Houston: Harpia, 2008)

Warnes, Alan, *The Pakistan Air Force, 1998 – 2008 A New Dawn* (Stamford: Key Publishing, 2009)

Willisch, Dr. Jürgen, *Mikoyan-Gurevich MiG-21F-13/U* (Arbeitsgemeinschaft Luftwaffe (AGL) e.V., 2004) (in German)

Aviation Archives 03/2008 Vol. 207

Articles from the magazines *FliegerRevue, FliegerRevue Extra, Air Forces Monthly* and *letectví + kosmonautika.*

Internet Sources (Selection)

http://www.afwing.com/intro/j-7/legend/(abridged Internet version of Aviation Archives 03 / 2008)

https://defence.pk/pdf/threads/mig-21s-f-7s-specifications-capabilities.297826/

https://www.scramble.nl/planning/orbats

https://avialatina.com.ar/los-que-no-fueron-parte-2/

https://www.key.aero/article/history-chengdu-f-7n-iranian-service

https://www.turkishdefencenews.com/bangladesh-supplies-teber-guidance-kit-from-turkiye/

https://www.fullaviacion.com.ar/2022/08/28/rd-93-desde-rusia-con-amor-2-entrega/

https://www.youtube.com/watch?v=BayjAFra_6U

ABOUT THE AUTHOR

Holger Müller

Born in 1968 in the former German Democratic Republic (GDR), Holger Müller was always an aviation enthusiast since his childhood. He completed his military service in the GDR Air Force from 1988 to 1990 as a MiG-21 technician. Since then, this subject has never left him – as evidenced by numerous related articles and books he has published. Müller has travelled to more than 20 user countries of the MiG-21 and J/F-7s fighters and the majority of his publications about this prolific family are based on his own research and photographic material.